THE HOLY SPIRIT AND CHRISTIAN EXPERIENCE

By MACK B. STOKES

GRADED PRESS
NASHVILLE, TENNESSEE

A publication of The United Methodist Church prepared by the
Board of Discipleship through the Section on Curriculum
Resources and published by Graded Press, the curriculum publishing
department of The United Methodist Publishing House,
201 Eighth Avenue, South, Nashville, Tennessee 37202. Printed
in the United States of America.

   Ewart G. Watts is editor of church school publications,
Section on Curriculum Resources, Board of Discipleship,
The United Methodist Church.
   Horace R. Weaver is editor of adult publications.
   Maxine C. Stout is manuscript editor.
   R. E. Osborne is book designer and illustrator.

Because paper is in short supply, paper stock may vary in
appearance within this book.

TO ELSIE PAULINE

CONTENTS

EPISCOPAL FOREWORD 9

PREFACE 13

INTRODUCTION
The Trinity: The Christian Understanding of God . . 15

THE BIBLICAL TEACHING
Chapter 1. Foundations in the Old Testament 21
Chapter 2. The Holy Spirit in Matthew, Mark, and
Luke 29
Chapter 3. Major Sources in the New Testament . . . 35

THE HOLY SPIRIT AND THE CHURCH
Chapter 4. The Holy Spirit and the Historic
Community of Faith 49
Chapter 5. The Holy Spirit and the Wesleyan
Heritage 61

THE HOLY SPIRIT AND PERSONAL SALVATION
Chapter 6. The Holy Spirit and the Human Spirit . . 73
Chapter 7. The Holy Spirit and the New Birth 79
Chapter 8. The Witness of the Spirit 87
Chapter 9. The Creative Power of the Spirit 95

THE HOLY SPIRIT AND THE CHRISTIAN LIFE

Chapter 10. The Holy Spirit and Christian Habits . . 107
Chapter 11. The Holy Spirit and the Concern for
Souls 113
Chapter 12. The Holy Spirit and Responsible
Living in Community 121
Chapter 13. The Holy Spirit and the Ecumenical
Spirit 129

THE HOLY SPIRIT AND AND THE
CHARISMATIC MOVEMENT

Chapter 14. The Holy Spirit and Speaking in
Tongues 137
Chapter 15. The Church's Response to Speaking in
Tongues 147
Chapter 16. The Holy Spirit and Divine Healing,
Exorcism, Psychic Phenomena, and
the Occult 159

SELECTED RESOURCES

A. Key Passages of Scripture 173
Old Testament
New Testament
B. Selected Books 174

EPISCOPAL FOREWORD

The General Conference of 1972 ordered the Council of Bishops to supervise the preparation of a study book "on the saving personal experience of Jesus Christ followed by the empowerment by the Holy Spirit for service to God and people." The General Conference further ordered the Council of Bishops to "give spiritual and administrative leadership" in the churchwide use of this book and in a series of associated efforts. The Council, through its Standing Committee on Teaching Concerns, commissioned Bishop Mack B. Stokes to write the study book and sought the assistance of the Section on Curriculum Resources of the Board of Discipleship in its publication and marketing. A Leader's Guide has been prepared and is available for use in conjunction with the study book.

In further response to the General Conference's mandate, the Council of Bishops, working with other appropriate United Methodist leadership, will lead a churchwide study of this book during 1975-76. Additional resource materials related to this study have also been prepared under the auspices of the Council of Bishops and are being published by Tidings.

I

A fresh discovery of the meaning of Christian experience and the power of the Holy Spirit seems to be of widespread interest throughout the church.

Some features of the current situation, however, are alarming to the spiritually timid. For example, the charismatic is emotional in a manner frightening to those not accustomed to this. It is as free and bold as the wind,

9

gaily uninhibited, attractively different, imbued with power that can grip personality and grapple with character. It is heady stuff for the parson or the pew-sitter who likes his religion served up in structured, orthodox form. But it is bringing excitement to the Christian community, producing many instances of conversion, re-creating interest in the Bible, laying redemptive and revolutionary hold upon worldly folk previously impervious to the voice of the church, and giving ample evidence that it is here to stay in our time.

The basic purpose of this study book is to guide this rediscovery of Christian experience and the power of the Holy Spirit into realistic and constructive channels pointing toward the further renewal of The United Methodist Church.

II

The bishops of The United Methodist Church willingly and gladly accept the role of leadership in this effort requested by the General Conference. The bishops have a deeply lodged desire to move beyond the purely administrative demands of their task and to occupy areas of influence more immediately spiritual and intellectual in nature. Actually this would represent a re-appropriation of one of the earliest functions of the episcopacy, dating back to the second century. Although the origins of the office are somewhat obscure, in those early years the bishop of a community was entrusted with the *cathedra*, or teaching chair, in succession to one who in his turn had been the holder of that chair. His function was to teach, interpret, and defend the faith; and his own intelligence, knowledge, and consecration were required to measure up to this apostolic responsibility. Surely it is past time for episcopal leadership, often tormented by the chores of administrative routine, to lay fresh hold upon its *historic teaching task*— for the good of its own soul and for the enlightenment of the Christian community.

One bishop, writing to recently appointed clergymen a few years ago, gave them this challenge: The people of our time seem to have lost sight of the fundamentals of the gospel. You must go out and find it for them and restore it to their lives.

This little volume is sent forth to The United Methodist Church by the Council of Bishops at a critical moment in the life and opportunity of God's people. It is sent with the sincere prayer that, through the combined leadership of bishops, pastors, and dedicated lay people, United Methodists in the 1970's may come to a new understanding and use of the power of Christian experience and the Holy Spirit.

The gratitude of the Council of Bishops is expressed to Bishop Stokes, formerly Franklin Nutting Parker Professor of Systematic Theology at Candler School of Theology, Emory University, for skillful handling of this commission.

EARL G. HUNT, JR., *Chairman*
Standing Committee on Teaching Concerns
The Council of Bishops
The United Methodist Church

Charlotte, North Carolina
August 15, 1974

PREFACE

For many years it was my privilege to teach a course on the doctrine of the Holy Spirit at the Candler School of Theology, Emory University. During those years of careful and prayerful study I came to see increasingly that the Holy Spirit's work is connected by divine policy with Jesus Christ's mission in the world. Wherever there are people, the Holy Spirit is present. But his distinctive work in the hearts of people does not come to full visibility apart from Jesus Christ and the community of faith that is charged with carrying out his mission.

This book has been in preparation for a number of years. One incentive for bringing it out now is the churches' new awareness of the Spirit's work. During these days when we hear so much talk about the Holy Spirit and some renewed signs of his presence and power, it seems fitting to bring together some basic affirmations growing out of the biblical revelation.

Another immediate incentive has been the desire of The United Methodist Church for such a study. The Council of Bishops was charged by the General Conference of 1972 with the responsibility of preparing a study on the Holy Spirit and Christian experience. The council, in turn, asked me to write the book in fulfillment of the mandate.

I am indebted to many people for assisting in the formation of the ideas of this book. Among them, of course, are my wife, Rose, and my daughter, Elsie, who have been considerate and understanding concerning those times of separation required by the work. Among those who have helped also are my many students at the Candler School of Theology who sat in my classes in large numbers and contributed to my thinking. My colleagues on the faculty there, though often representing vastly different perspectives from my own, enabled me to receive insights that would not have come without their stimulating ideas.

A special word of appreciation needs to be expressed to the Council of Bishops of The United Methodist Church which had the confidence to entrust me with this responsibility. My thanks too are due my friends and colleagues, Bishops Earl G. Hunt, Jr., and Wayne K. Clymer, the former for his leadership as chairman of the committee on teaching concerns and the latter for reading the manuscript with care and making numerous helpful suggestions. I am grateful to the United Methodists of Mississippi for respecting my hours of study amid many other duties so that this work could be completed on schedule.

My gratitude goes to Horace R. Weaver, Executive Editor of the Department of Adult Publications, Section on Curriculum Resources, for sensitive and helpful collaboration in the project; and to Maxine C. Stout for her painstaking and perceptive editorial work on the manuscript.

Last, but by no means least, I am specially grateful to Mrs. Hattie Pearl Decell for her patience and skill in typing the manuscript again and again, when necessary, in order to present a work as nearly perfect as possible.

MACK B. STOKES
Bishop of The United Methodist Church

Jackson, Mississippi
August 1, 1974

INTRODUCTION

The Trinity: The Christian Understanding of God

The circle in this symbol for the Trinity denotes
eternity; the three equal arcs symbolizing the three
persons of the Trinity are interwoven in a manner
that indicates their indivisibility.

The historic doctrine of the Trinity expresses the distinctively Christian understanding of God. According to it, there is one God who is Father, Son, and Holy Spirit. This doctrine, though not written into the creeds for several centuries after Christ, was implied in the New Testament and affirmed by the early Christians.

The purpose here is not to give a detailed account of the Trinity. Rather, it is to prepare the way for our discussion on the Holy Spirit. Since God is understood by us as Father, Son, and Holy Spirit, some introductory remarks on the interrelationships of these three may prove helpful.

Origin of the Doctrine of the Trinity

The doctrine of the Trinity is not found in the Hebrew religion. While there are other trinities in various religions, these are vastly different from the Christian doctrine of God. Nevertheless, some scholars have mistakenly tried to show that the Christian Trinity came from these other religions.

For example, among the ancient Egyptians there was the "trinity" known as Osiris, Isis, and Horus. The Sumerians, Romans, Hindus, and others have had their triads. The Hindu "trinity" consists of Brahma, Vishnu, and Siva, which are different manifestations of the impersonal Brahman.

All efforts to trace the Christian Trinity to other religions have failed because they were not true to the actual development of Christian teaching and experience. Some scholars even tried to show that the Christian doctrine of the Trinity arose because the number *three* has had special significance since primitive times. But no such theory makes sense to those who understand how the idea of the Trinity actually came about. Still others have referred the doctrine of the Trinity to a supposed threefold root of religion, namely, nature worship, the cult of the dead, and the belief in the supreme Being.

The only reason for mentioning these strange views is to emphasize the fact that the Christian teaching on the Trinity arose out of distinctive events in Christian history. From the Hebrew heritage came the idea of God as Creator and Sustainer of the universe. In addition, the earliest Christians found themselves confronted by God in Jesus Christ, although it took some time for the profound depths of this reality to emerge.

In the end, however, the real reason for speaking of God as the Son was that in Jesus Christ God revealed himself and worked mightily in the lives of those earliest Christians. Similarly, the real reason for thinking of God as Holy Spirit was that Jesus promised the power of the Spirit, and Jesus' followers received that power. They felt God's presence in the marvelous outpouring of the Holy Spirit at Pentecost and in the continuing communities of faith. The promise of Jesus and of the risen Lord was fulfilled.

Views of the Doctrine of the Trinity

The Trinity may be thought of in two ways. One is theoretical; the other, practical.

Theoretically, Christians have never been able to clarify fully the doctrine that God is Three-in-One—Father, Son, and Holy Spirit. They have recognized the profound mystery of the divine Being. Perhaps all we can say is that within God's mysterious depths are three basic natures that, though distinct, are dynamically interrelated in the divine Being. On this level the doctrine of the Trinity is affirmed as a mystery, and the depth of God's being is beyond our understanding. (See Romans 11:33-36.)

From a practical standpoint we can understand the Trinity in terms of the three most dynamic and creative ways in which God is related to his children. First, God is Creator and Sustainer of the universe and humankind. Second, God is Redeemer. Third, God is the life-giving Presence through Christ. We need to know that God created the universe and that he made us and placed us in it. We need to know that God is gracious and gives himself in redemptive love. We need to know that God is near, available, presently at work to magnify Jesus as Lord and to bind us together in worship, understanding, and service.

A major difference between a unitarian and trinitarian is that the unitarian is unable to specify clearly how God relates himself to us. And when we do not understand *specifically* how God is related to us, we do not know exactly how to respond to him. This cuts off the flow of the divine processes in and through us and leaves us largely on our own, unaided by the divine redemptive and creative grace.

As important as any aspect of the Christian religion is its claim that God has revealed himself as the One who has *taken the initiative in our behalf.* He not only created us, he has come to our aid. He has revealed the specific ways in which he is dealing with us. He summons us to respond in repentance, faith, and obedience to his gracious initiative. The Holy Spirit is God at work in us *now*.

As we reflect on the Holy Spirit in the chapters that follow, we need to keep in mind the larger Christian understanding of God as Father, Son, and Holy Spirit, for there is always the danger of unitarianism. Sometimes unitarian

17

thinking stresses God the Father; sometimes, God the Son; sometimes, God the Holy Spirit. It may so emphasize Jesus Christ as to obscure God as Father and Holy Spirit. Similarly, it may get so carried away with the Holy Spirit as to push into the background the idea of God the Father and the Son.

Having noted these dangers in an imbalanced view of the Trinity, we may now consider the Christian doctrine of the Holy Spirit.

THE
BIBLICAL TEACHING

1

Foundations in the Old Testament

One of the most distinctive themes of the Bible is that God takes the initiative to warn and bless his children. He wants them to have all the benefits of his grace. This biblical theme, which comes to supreme utterance in the New Testament, distinguishes Christianity from all other religions. No other reveals such an exalted and passionate determination on God's part to give himself for persons and for their salvation.

The Bible teaches that God's self-giving love becomes real in us by the presence and power of the Holy Spirit. Therefore, we need to understand the Holy Spirit and how he works in us.

Our basic guide here is the Bible, and particularly the New Testament. But, since the Old Testament prepares the way for the New, we need to consider how it leads up to the teaching on the Holy Spirit in the New Testament. In this chapter we shall consider the background in the Old Testament. In the next two chapters we shall turn to the directives that are given to us in the New Testament.

The Spirit of God is mentioned in the first creation story as "moving over the face of the waters." The suggestion is that the Spirit was involved in the creation and ordering of the universe. Thus the Spirit is a dynamic and creative Being—Divine Energy, the origin of all created life. In the Book of Job we read:

"The Spirit of God has made me,
and the breath of the Almighty gives me life." (33:4)

Dimensions of the Spirit

In the Old Testament generally the word *spirit* refers to God as he acts in the world. It reflects God's determination to use human history as a base of operations. Deism—the theory that God created the universe and left it to run by itself—is wholly alien to the Bible, which tells us that the Spirit of God is radically involved in the affairs of humankind. At the same time, interestingly enough, we find no trace of pantheism in the Old Testament; that is, God is not identified with the universe or with objects in nature, nor are people thought of as tiny parts of God.

The teaching on the Spirit as God actively at work in human history stands in contrast to those views of God as being totally above and beyond this earthly scene. Similarly, it stands in contrast to the idea of a static deity. For example, Plato's understanding of God led him to deny the kind of divine involvement in human history and destiny of which the biblical writers speak. According to the main direction of Plato's thought, to be active is to be in some measure deficient. Since God is perfect, and since, according to Plato, perfection implies changelessness, detachment, and uninvolvement, the biblical idea of the God who cares would have been viewed by Plato as unsound.

We should note in passing that sometimes the Spirit of God was said to act almost arbitrarily, without regard to moral aims. Besides the tremendous feats of Samson, the Spirit many times acted in extraordinary, abnormal, and apparently arbitrary ways. The ecstatic experiences of Ezekiel were attributed to the Spirit. (Ezekiel 3:12-15; 8:3; 11:1, 24; 43:5) Thus the Spirit of God was seen as the unpredictable and irresistible power of God.

These incidents, however, are secondary to the over-whelming concern for righteousness. The Spirit of God was not essentially understood as raw power. Rather, it was understood as power with moral force.

> "Woe to the rebellious children," says the LORD,
>   "who carry out a plan, but not mine;
> and who make a league, but not of my spirit,
>   that they may add sin to sin." (Isaiah 30:1)

This moral quality is particularly evident in some of the psalms.

> "Create in me a clean heart, O God,
>   and put a new and right spirit within me.
> Cast me not away from thy presence,
>   and take not thy holy Spirit from me."
>   (Psalms 51:10-11)

Again,

> "Teach me to do thy will,
>   for thou art my God!
> Let thy good spirit lead me
>   on a level path!" (143:10)

Many of the prophets joined in this theme. In the Book of Isaiah, for example, we read as follows of the Spirit's work:

> "The Spirit of the Lord GOD is upon me,
>   because the LORD has anointed me
> to bring good tidings to the afflicted;
>   he has sent me to bind up the brokenhearted,
> to proclaim liberty to the captives,
>   and the opening of the prison to those who are bound;
> To proclaim the year of the LORD's favor,
>   and the day of vengeance of our God;
>   to comfort all who mourn." (61:1-2)

The prophet Micah also emphasizes the moral force of the Spirit when he says:

"But as for me, I am filled with power,
with the Spirit of the LORD,
and with justice and might,
to declare to Jacob his transgression
and to Israel his sin." (3:8)

Zechariah brings this theme to magnificent utterance in the familiar words: "Not by might, nor by power, but by my Spirit, says the LORD of hosts." (4:6)

The Spirit Deals With People

Many religious thinkers have felt they were giving God a special glory by viewing him as disassociated from the world and its creatures. But the biblical writers would have none of this. Unapologetically they spoke of God as Creator and Sustainer of the universe. Boldly they declared that the Spirit of God deals with people.

● Sometimes the Spirit gives persons special skills, including artistic ability. Of Bezalel the son of Uri we read: "I have filled him with the Spirit of God, with ability and intelligence, with knowledge and all craftsmanship, to devise artistic designs, to work in gold, silver, and bronze, in cutting stones for setting, and in carving wood, for work in every craft." (Exodus 31:3-5; see also 35:31-35.)

● At other times the Spirit gives people leadership ability. The Spirit that was upon Moses was to be put upon the seventy elders so they could help Moses "bear the burden of the people." (Numbers 11:17)

Joshua was to succeed Moses because the Spirit was in him. (Numbers 27:18) When the Spirit of the Lord came upon Othniel, he judged Israel. (Judges 3:10) Again and again we read of the Spirit's action in relation to the leaders of Israel. "But the Spirit of the LORD took possession of Gideon." (6:34) "Then the Spirit of the LORD came upon Jephthah." (11:29) Even Samson's giant strength came from the Spirit of God. (14:6, 19; 15:14)

Samuel said to Saul, "Then the spirit of the LORD will come mightily upon you, and you shall prophesy with them and be turned into another man." (1 Samuel 10:6) And the Spirit of God came with power upon Saul. (11:6)

We are told also that "the spirit of the LORD came mightily upon David." (1 Samuel 16:13) David's last words were, "The Spirit of the LORD speaks by me." (2 Samuel 23:1-2)

The Spirit of God, as we see, set people apart for leadership and gave them special powers for being effective leaders. Indeed, the only genuine leaders in Israel were those under the influence of the Spirit.

In no prophet was the work of the Spirit more vivid than in Ezekiel. The Spirit, he says, fell upon him (11:5); and again and again he tells of the Spirit lifting him up (3:12, 14; 8:3; 11:1, 24; 43:5). He refers to the Lord's commission in these words: "And when he spoke to me, the Spirit entered into me and set me upon my feet; and I heard him speaking to me. And he said to me, 'Son of man, I send you to the people of Israel, to a nation of rebels, who have rebelled against me; they and their fathers have transgressed against me to this very day.' " (2:2-3)

Then Ezekiel declared God's promise of the Spirit to the people. "A new heart I will give you, and a new spirit I will put within you; and I will take out of your flesh the heart of stone and give you a heart of flesh. And I will put my spirit within you, and cause you to walk in my statutes and be careful to observe my ordinances." (36: 26-27)

● While it is true that the Spirit of God made himself known most clearly in the prophets, the Spirit was said to be present also in the people of Israel as a group. The Lord made a covenant with his people, saying, "My spirit which is upon you, and my words which I have put in your mouth, shall not depart out of your mouth, or out of the mouth of your children, or out of the mouth of your children's children, says the LORD, from this time forth and for evermore." (Isaiah 59:21; see also Nehemiah 9:20; Haggai 2:5.)

As one writer puts it, the Spirit had been guiding the nation of Israel since the time of the Exodus.

> "But they rebelled
>   and grieved his holy Spirit;
> therefore he turned to be their enemy,
>   and himself fought against them.
> Then he remembered the days of old,
>   of Moses his servant.

25

Where is he who brought up out of the sea
   the shepherds of his flock?
Where is he who put in the midst of them
   his holy Spirit,
who caused his glorious arm
   to go at the right hand of Moses,
who divided the waters before them
   to make for himself an everlasting name,
   who led them through the depths?"
                    (Isaiah 63:10-13)

Hope for the Future

One more dimension of the Spirit's activity in the Old
Testament needs to be mentioned, namely, its relation to
the future. We read of the vision of the Spirit's initiative
in the work of the Messiah to come:

"There shall come forth a shoot
   from the stump of Jesse,
and a branch shall grow out of his roots.
   And the Spirit of the LORD shall rest upon him . . . ."
                    (Isaiah 11:1-2)

We read also of the magnificent vision of the outpouring
of the Spirit to form the new Israel. (Israel 44:3) The
supremely representative passage on this vision is Ezekiel
37:1-14. The Spirit set the prophet amid the dry bones
in the valley (referring to Israel captive in Babylon), and
Ezekiel was given the vision of the new Israel. The Lord
said to him: "And you shall know that I am the LORD,
when I open your graves, and raise you from your graves,
O my people. And I will put my Spirit within you, and
you shall live." (37:13-14; see also 39:29.)

The greatest vision in the Old Testament regarding the
Spirit's activity in the future is described in the Book of
Joel. There the prophet is given the vision of the outpour-
ing of the Spirit on *all humankind*.

"And it shall come to pass afterward,
   that I will pour out my spirit on all flesh;
your sons and your daughters shall prophesy,
   your old men shall dream dreams,

and your young men shall see visions.
Even upon the menservants and maidservants
in those days, I will pour out my spirit."
(2:28-29)

Then the prophet adds, "And it shall come to pass that all who call upon the name of the LORD shall be delivered." (2:32)

These words are significant because they envision *the universal sweep of the Spirit's activity*. The Spirit's work not only is worldwide, it reaches beyond our human distinctions of culture and status to place all people, whether men or women or servants or masters, under the possible sway of the Spirit.

Summary

We may summarize the teaching of the Old Testament on the Spirit by drawing six conclusions:

First, the Spirit of God is understood as the medium of God's involvement in human history. He cares, he is concerned, he acts in history.

Second, the Spirit acts in many different ways—sometimes quite unpredictably—but primarily he acts to achieve moral goals in the lives of people.

Third, the Spirit is particularly active in and through selected individuals, such as Moses, Joshua, Samuel, David, Ezekiel.

Fourth, the Spirit is also in some sense present in the people of Israel as a whole; he acts to maintain the identity and heritage of Israel.

Fifth, the Spirit is viewed as inaugurating the messianic era yet to come when all people everywhere, regardless of station or rank or nationality, may receive the outpouring of the Spirit. This promise is to be fulfilled.

Finally, in the Old Testament the work of the Spirit is preparatory. *It is not clearly and fully described.* It awaits fulfillment in the New Testament. The two words *Holy Spirit* are seldom used together in the Old Testament. When they are, they do not reflect their use in the New Testament. As we shall see, the full clarification of the mission of the Holy Spirit was not possible until the work of Jesus Christ had been completed.

2

The Holy Spirit in Matthew, Mark, and Luke

Symbols for the Evangelists are suggested by the "living creatures" in Revelation 4:7. The winged man symbolizes Matthew whose Gospel dwells more on the humanity of Jesus than the other Gospels do. The lion (king of beasts) stands for royalty—the kingship of Jesus Christ as presented by Mark. The ox (often a sacrificial animal) symbolizes Luke whose Gospel stresses the sacrifice of Jesus Christ on the cross.

Until the past decade the doctrine of the Holy Spirit was one of the most neglected vital teachings of the Christian religion. When not neglected, it was almost sure to be misunderstood. Why the neglect? Why the misunderstanding? Chiefly because of a failure to follow the directives of the New Testament concerning the Holy Spirit.

Some have thought of the work of the Holy Spirit in terms of inner impressions, hunches, suggestions, impulses. Others have thought in terms of outer signs, speaking in tongues, using unusual gestures, making loud noises, and the like. Still others, on a more sophisticated level, have identified the work of the Holy Spirit with the higher aspirations of people toward goodness, beauty, and truth. All sorts of other views have been held, but these will suffice to show the need for some authentic foundation for our thinking about the Holy Spirit.

That foundation is the New Testament. The Old Testament prepares the way, but it does not describe sufficiently

THE HOLY SPIRIT AND CHRISTIAN EXPERIENCE

the distinctive mission of the Holy Spirit. Against this background we turn now to the teaching of the New Testament as our primary source and guide.

We might think it strange at first that the so-called Synoptic Gospels (Matthew, Mark, and Luke) have relatively little to say about the Holy Spirit. This is especially true of Mark. But, on second thought, this is quite understandable because those Gospel writers were concentrating on Jesus. Their primary goal was to tell about Jesus, to declare his message, and to interpret his life, death, and resurrection.

In the Life of Jesus

Matthew and Luke make special reference to the Holy Spirit in relation to Jesus' birth and life.

● We may begin by noting some references to the Holy Spirit as preparing the way for Jesus' birth. According to both Matthew and Luke the Holy Spirit acted in the conception of Jesus. (Matthew 1:18, 20; Luke 1:35) The Holy Spirit thus is seen as taking the initiative in the beginning of the new era of the kingdom of God in Jesus Christ—the New Creation, the New Humanity through Christ.

In Luke 1 and 2 the Holy Spirit gives the vision of the coming One. For example, Zechariah, the father of John the Baptist, was "filled with the Holy Spirit" and prophesied, saying,

> "Blessed be the Lord God of Israel,
> for he has visited and redeemed his people,
> and has raised up a horn of salvation for us
> in the house of his servant David." (1:68-69)

Then, linking this babe, John, with the Messiah, Zechariah went on:

"And you, child, will be called the prophet of the Most
  High;
for you will go before the Lord to prepare his ways,
to give knowledge of salvation to his people
in the forgiveness of their sins,
through the tender mercy of our God,
when the day shall dawn upon us from on high

to give light to those who sit in darkness and in the shadow
of death,
to guide our feet into the way of peace." (1:76-79)

Similarly, when Elizabeth, herself with child, heard and
saw Mary, she was filled with the Holy Spirit and ex-
claimed in a loud cry: "Blessed are you among women, and
blessed is the fruit of your womb! And why is this granted
me, that the mother of my Lord should come to me?"
(1:41-43)

The Holy Spirit came upon Simeon, a righteous man in
Jerusalem who was looking for "the consolation of Israel."
"And it had been revealed to him by the Holy Spirit that
he should not see death before he had seen the Lord's
Christ. And inspired by the Spirit he came into the temple;
and when the parents brought in the child Jesus, to do
for him according to the custom of the law, he took him
up in his arms and blessed God and said,

"Lord, now lettest thou thy servant depart in peace,
according to thy word;
for mine eyes have seen thy salvation
which thou hast prepared in the presence of all peoples,
a light for revelation to the Gentiles,
and for glory to thy people Israel." (Luke 2:26-32)

In these passages the theme emerges concerning *the in-
herent and indissoluble connection between the mission of
Jesus and the mission of the Holy Spirit.*

We see this connection also in the work of the Holy Spirit
in certain events in Jesus' life as described in the Gospels.

● At Jesus' baptism the Holy Spirit came upon him.
(Matthew 3:16; Mark 1:10; Luke 3:22) As the Spirit de-
scended upon him like a dove, a voice from heaven was
saying, "Thou art my beloved Son; with thee I am well
pleased." (Mark 1:11)

The contrast between the Spirit's work in John the Baptist and in Jesus is worth noting. In the case of John, the
Spirit simply carried forward the preparatory work of the
Old Testament prophets. He was the last in the line of those
who were led by the Spirit to prepare the way for the

31

Messiah. Thus it was no accident that Luke referred to the words of Isaiah in connection with John's mission:

"The voice of one crying in the wilderness:
Prepare the way of the Lord,
make his paths straight." (Luke 3:4)

John recognized all this about himself. For when the multitudes asked whether or not he might be the Christ, he answered: "I baptize you with water; but there is one to come who is mightier than I. I am not fit to unfasten his shoes. He will baptize you with the Holy Spirit and with fire." (Luke 3:16, *The New English Bible*)[1]

At the time of Jesus' baptism, then, the Holy Spirit was especially active. Just as he had inaugurated the new era through Jesus' unique birth, at Jesus' baptism he was present in a special way at the beginning of the official ministry of our Lord.

• The Spirit was present also at the time of Jesus' temptations. "The Spirit immediately drove him out into the wilderness. And he was in the wilderness forty days, tempted by Satan . . . ." (Mark 1:12-13, see also Matthew 4:1; Luke 4:1.) This too has special significance, for not even Jesus could become fully identified with our common humanity without the profoundest encounters with temptation. It says something to all of us that "in every respect [he] has been tempted as we are, yet without sin." (Hebrews 4:15) John Milton was right when he said in *Paradise Regained* that unless our Lord had won the victory during those early days in the wilderness, there could have been no Gethsemane, Calvary, or Easter.

• Similarly, the Spirit was present with Jesus in his continuing ministry. "And Jesus returned in the power of the Spirit into Galilee, and a report concerning him went out through all the surrounding country." (Luke 4:14)

When the seventy people whom Jesus sent out to evangelize returned, they reported what had happened. Jesus rejoiced in the Holy Spirit and said: "I thank thee, Father,

---

[1] From *The New English Bible*, © The Delegates of the Oxford University Press and the Syndics of the Cambridge University Press 1961, 1970. Reprinted by permission.

Lord of heaven and earth, that thou hast hidden these things from the wise and understanding and revealed them to babes." (Luke 10:21)

The earliest Christians evidently assumed that the Master's good deeds and healing power were linked with the Holy Spirit. Peter is quoted as saying to Cornelius and the others, "You know the word which he [God] sent to Israel . . . how God anointed Jesus of Nazareth with the Holy Spirit and with power; how he went about doing good and healing all that were oppressed by the devil, for God was with him." (Acts 10:36, 38)

Jesus' Prophetic Role

The Spirit was also manifested in the prophetic role of Jesus. Early in his public ministry he went to the synagogue at Nazareth on the sabbath day and read these words from the Book of Isaiah:

"The Spirit of the Lord is upon me,
because he has anointed me to preach good news to the poor.
He has sent me to proclaim release to the captives
and recovering of sight to the blind,
to set at liberty those who are oppressed,
to proclaim the acceptable year of the Lord."

(Luke 4:18-19)

Then Jesus added: "Today this scripture has been fulfilled in your hearing." (4:21) Thus in Jesus Christ the Spirit moved with compassionate concern for justice and liberation for the oppressed.

From time to time, also, Jesus promised the outpouring of the Spirit upon his followers. He told them that the heavenly Father wanted to give them the Holy Spirit (Luke 11:13) and that the power of the Holy Spirit would be available in times of need (Matthew 10:19-20; Mark 13:11; Luke 12:11-12). This is supremely true in the risen Lord's summons to evangelize the world. He said, "And behold, I send the promise of my Father upon you; but stay in the city, until you are clothed with power from on high." (Luke 24:49; see also Acts 1:4-5.)

In his great commission the risen Lord said, "Go therefore and make disciples of all nations, baptizing them in the name of the Father and of the Son and of the Holy Spirit." (Matthew 28:19) Here we move beyond the idea of the Holy Spirit as available power to the idea of the Holy Spirit in his relationships within the divine Being. The Trinity is thus the theological basis for world evangelization.

Two major conclusions are to be drawn from this brief survey of the Holy Spirit in Matthew, Mark, and Luke.

First, the primary interest of each of these Gospel writers was to present a valid, convincing view of Jesus and his message and ministry. Each one wanted to tell the story of Jesus and of God's good news so that people would repent and trust.

A second conclusion is quite unmistakable, namely, that the unique mission of Jesus Christ as Lord and Redeemer is attended from beginning to end by the presence and power of the Holy Spirit. Even though this theme is not extensively developed in these three Gospels, it is there. This fact gives added weight to the clear directives that will be discussed as we turn in the next chapter to John's Gospel, to the Acts of the Apostles, and to Paul's writings.

3

Major Sources in the New Testament

Since the eagle soars high in the heavens, the winged eagle denotes John and his emphasis on the divinity of Jesus Christ.

In the New Testament three sources on the work of the Holy Spirit overshadow all other passages. These references are to be taken by Christians as the primary authoritative guides regarding the mission of the Holy Spirit. The three sources are (1) Jesus' teachings as recorded in John's Gospel; (2) the happenings at Pentecost as recorded in Acts 2; and (3) certain inspired and judicious utterances of the apostle Paul.

The Holy Spirit in John's Gospel

In the Fourth Gospel certain preliminary passages relative to the Holy Spirit should be noted at the outset. One of these is the story of Jesus and Nicodemus. (3:1-8) Here is the magnificent vision of the new birth made possible by the Spirit: "That which is born of the flesh is flesh, and that which is born of the Spirit is spirit." (3:6) We see mystery here and also re-creative power. Jesus also referred to God's *measureless* gift of the Spirit. (3:34) One gets the impression that Jesus was speaking of the work of the Spirit when he said to the Samaritan woman, ". . . whoever drinks of the water that I shall give him will never thirst; the water that I shall give him will become in him a spring of water welling up to eternal life." (4:14; see also 7:38-39.)

We are left with a profound sense of the superabounding work of the Spirit. The Master wanted us to know of the vast resources of God through the Spirit.

The Key Passage

In John 16:7-15 we find the most important teaching on the Holy Spirit recorded in that Gospel.

● In other passages Jesus is quoted in somewhat comparable ways. For example, in 14:16-17 we read: "And I will pray the Father, and he will give you another Counselor, to be with you for ever, even the Spirit of truth, whom the world cannot receive, because it neither sees him nor knows him; you know him, for he dwells with you, and will be in you." These words contain the promise of the Spirit, although they do not outline his primary mission. He was to be in some sense the Spirit of truth; and these verses assume that he would dwell, not in everyone, but in those intimately associated with Jesus.

Further clarification is found when Jesus said, "These things I have spoken to you, while I am still with you. But the Counselor, the Holy Spirit, whom the Father will send in my name, he will teach you all things, and bring to your remembrance all that I have said to you." (14:25-26) Here the teaching work of the Holy Spirit is emphasized, and the direction of that teaching is indicated. The Holy Spirit would not disconnect his mission from the work of Jesus Christ. He would enable the disciples to remember what Jesus had said.

The Holy Spirit's unique mission is clarified further still in 15:26, where Jesus said, "But when the Counselor comes, whom I shall send to you from the Father, even the Spirit of truth, who proceeds from the Father, he will bear witness to me; and you also are witnesses, because you have been with me from the beginning." Here the Spirit is understood clearly as bearing witness to Jesus.

● All these teachings, and more, are brought together in John 16:7-15, which is this Gospel's great passage on the work of the Holy Spirit. Jesus said to his disciples:

"Nevertheless I tell you the truth: it is to your advantage that I go away, for if I do not go away, the Counselor will not come to you; but if I go, I will send him to you. And when he comes, he will convince the world concerning sin and righteousness and judgment: concerning sin, because they do not believe in me; concerning righteousness, because I go to the Father, and you will see me no more; concerning judgment, because the ruler of this world is judged.

"I have yet many things to say to you, but you cannot bear them now. When the Spirit of truth comes, he will guide you into all the truth; for he will not speak on his own authority, but whatever he hears he will speak, and he will declare to you the things that are to come. He will glorify me, for he will take what is mine and declare it to you. All that the Father has is mine; therefore I said that he will take what is mine and declare it to you."

● This passage has five thoughts of the utmost importance.

First, the Holy Spirit's coming had to await the completion of Jesus' mission. "If I do not go away," said Jesus, "the Counselor will not come to you." This was suggested earlier in John's Gospel where the author says, "Now this he said about the Spirit, which those who believed in him were to receive; for as yet the Spirit had not been given, because Jesus was not yet glorified." (7:39)

Second, Jesus made it clear that he was the one who would send the Holy Spirit through the Father. In substance, this is the same as praying to the Father to send the Spirit. (14:16) His coming, then, would be to carry forward Jesus' mission in the world. We are not altogether clear what is meant by the Holy Spirit's work of convincing the world concerning sin, righteousness, and judgment. But the implication is that just as Jesus did these things during his earthly ministry, so the Holy Spirit will continue to do them by lifting up Jesus Christ in the world.

Third, this passage (16:7-15) clearly states that the Holy Spirit's unique mission is to magnify Jesus Christ. "He will glorify me, for he will take what is mine and declare it to you." This should be tied to the words, "he will guide you into all the truth." When the Holy Spirit is spoken of as the "Spirit of truth," this does not refer to philosophical, scientific, or historical truth. The Holy Spirit does not function as an encyclopedia or as a course in science or in

37

reflective thinking. Rather, he will guide people into *all the truth they need for their souls' salvation in Jesus Christ.* The Holy Spirit will glorify Jesus Christ. And the statement that "he will declare to you the things that are to come" would seem to refer, among other things, to the ultimate triumph of righteousness under the lordship of Jesus Christ.

Fourth, the work of the Holy Spirit is *incognito.* That is, he does not proclaim himself. He does not come bearing his own message. The Holy Spirit "will take what is mine," said Jesus, "and declare it to you." (16:14) The Holy Spirit is self-effacing in all that he does. His one great concern is to nurture within history the new creation, the new era of the kingdom of God in and through Jesus Christ.

Fifth, one of the primary features of the Holy Spirit's concern to magnify Jesus Christ is his *teaching* ministry. This has to do chiefly with *communicating* who Jesus was, what his message was, and what his life, death, and resurrection mean in the inauguration of God's new era.

The directives here are clear. Jesus himself made it forever impossible to separate the mission of the Holy Spirit from his own great work as Lord and Savior.

The Holy Spirit and Pentecost

Most people who read about the first Christian Pentecost are likely to stop with the first four verses of Acts 2. While those verses are of utmost importance, the whole chapter is necessary in order to understand the deeper dimensions of what has been called "an eternal moment in the destiny of mankind." We shall begin with 2:1-4 and then move on to other key verses in that chapter.

● At first we are struck with the unusual happenings. Suddenly there was a sound from heaven "like the rush of a mighty wind." And there appeared "tongues as of fire, distributed and resting on each one of them." They were all filled with the Holy Spirit and "began to speak in other tongues" (that is, foreign languages).

Were these events all that happened? Were they the deepest dimensions of the experience of those earliest Christians at Pentecost? To both questions the answer has to be No. To be sure, those outward signs were important at that time and place. They served as confirming signs of the extraordinary presence and power of the Holy Spirit.

That particular moment in history, in a true sense, marked the *real beginning of the community of faith* that was ever afterward to bear the name of Jesus Christ.

● When we read farther into Acts and note what Peter said, we begin to see the deeper meaning of Pentecost.

Who was this Peter? Remember that even though he may have said to Jesus, "You are the Christ, the Son of the living God" (Matthew 16:16), he did not really understand or deeply believe what he was saying. Later, in the presence of a servant girl, he denied that he had had anything to do with Jesus. (26:69-75) In other words, when Jesus was arrested, mocked, and tortured, Peter had denied him three times.

Look at that same man after the outpouring of the Holy Spirit at Pentecost. A vast multitude had gathered, possibly in the Temple area. Those who had received the outpouring of the Holy Spirit with Peter were there with him. And he stood forth to speak. The magnificent setting of the Temple area, with its massive colonnades, would have made a most impressive background for what Peter had to say. In this area Jesus' crucifixion had been plotted. Not far away was the place where Peter had trembled and in cowardice had denied his Lord.

Peter now lifted up his voice and addressed the multitude. What did he say? He said that what the prophet Joel had predicted about the outpouring of the Spirit had become a reality. (Acts 2:17-21) He went on to talk about Jesus, his life, death, and resurrection. (2:22-24) He tied all this into what David had said. (2:25-31) Then he spoke of Jesus' apostles as witnesses to the risen Lord and to the fact that through this exalted Lord the Holy Spirit had been poured out on his followers. (2:32-33) Peter gave this extraordinary witness: "Let all the house of Israel therefore know assuredly that God has made him both Lord and Christ, this Jesus whom you crucified." (2:36)

When the people asked, "Brethren, what shall we do?" Peter said, "Repent, and be baptized every one of you in the name of Jesus Christ for the forgiveness of your sins; and you shall receive the gift of the Holy Spirit." (2:38) We may note that he did not say there would be the rushing of a mighty wind or "tongues as of fire" resting on them, nor did he promise that they would speak in foreign languages. He simply said that through repentance, baptism, and faith in Jesus' name they would receive the gift of the Holy Spirit. He made no mention of outward signs.

One thing is sure: Peter was speaking to a multitude of people most of whom already knew something of Jesus through his recent presence and deeds among them. Some had heard him preach; and some had been healed by him. Some had been in the mob that had cried for Barabbas and said, "Away with this man [Jesus]!" "Crucify him!" (Luke 23:18, 25)

They Received the Spirit

Through their crucified and risen Lord the presence and power of God had been experienced by this band of Christians. This had been made possible by another event of overwhelming significance, namely, their minds were so wonderfully *illuminated* by the Holy Spirit that they grasped for the first time, in any settled way, the revealed truth that Jesus Christ was indeed the God-appointed Savior of the world and the Inaugurator of the new era. The Spirit of truth had opened their minds to comprehend the one indispensable reality. Ever after that they had no lingering doubts. Threats of prison or torture or persecution could not deter Peter and the others. Their commitment was sealed; they were filled with the power of the Spirit.

● Let us get the full picture. In Acts 2:1 we read: "When the day of Pentecost had come, they were all together in one place." Who were "they"? This is important, for the Holy Spirit did not act indiscriminately.

Why did not the Holy Spirit fill a group of dedicated scholars at Plato's academy near Athens? Some of them were high-minded and even spiritually inclined. Or, why did he not pour out his power upon those in the Essene community at Qumran? They were dedicated, determined to withdraw from the world, and given to spirituality. The answer is that the people in these other groups were not given the Holy Spirit *because they did not know who Jesus was.*

● On the other hand, the moment we ask who were gathered together at that first Christian outpouring of the Spirit, we *know* who they were. *They were persons who had been with Jesus.*

We can almost hear them, in between their prayers and hymns, talking about Jesus. They shared in a holy memory of what Jesus had said and done. One of them might have said, "Do you remember when he told us, 'I am the light of the world'?" Then someone would add, "Yes, and remember when he said, 'You are the light of the world'?" One after another repeated some saying or referred to an incident. "You remember Zacchaeus." "Yes, and what about blind Bartimaeus!" "You remember the story of the prodigal son." "And the parable of the sower." "Oh, and what he prayed in agony on the cross." So it went on and on.

The Holy Spirit stirred up and quickened their common memory with so many of Jesus' sayings and deeds that *they were prepared to receive* their risen Lord into their hearts. He was the supreme reality in their midst. The world was pushed into the background, Jesus was magnified.

Add to this a vivid awareness of Jesus' resurrection. They were the ones who shared the holy memory of Jesus as he had lived and died so recently. They also were the ones who saw the empty tomb and who beheld again and again their risen Lord. Jesus was alive. Risen! They knew it, for they had seen and heard for themselves. (Imagine for a moment the powerful impact of Jesus' resurrection.)

This leads us to the overarching conclusion that that group of people—and that group only—was prepared to receive the power of the Holy Spirit at that eternal moment in the destiny of humankind.

● Besides these explanatory facts, the people at that first Christian Pentecost shared in a common understanding of who Jesus was in the light of Scripture (the Old Testament). These people—and this was true later of Paul—interpreted Jesus as the *promised Messiah*. Jesus was not understood as coming into the world like a bolt out of the blue. His coming had been preceded by long centuries of preparation through the history and prophets of Israel. God, in his infinite love and wisdom, had acted in their time to mark the beginning of the new era of grace. Paul, though not present in that group, caught the spirit of it later when he said, "But when the time had fully come, God sent forth his Son . . ." (Galatians 4:4)

● One more factor needs to be lifted up. Those who shared in that outpouring had heard Jesus *promise* them the Holy Spirit. They had heard his great commission to be his witnesses in Jerusalem and in all Judea and Samaria and to the end of the earth. (Acts 1:4-5, 8) But they were not to go until they had received the power God had promised. Therefore the atmosphere was charged with expectancy.

Summary of Acts 2

First, the more unusual events that occurred were secondary compared to the mysterious release of the power of the Holy Spirit. They were accompanying factors only; they were not indispensable. Yet they reveal to all with ears to hear that the Holy Spirit may break forth in great moments and surprising ways to magnify Jesus Christ and to carry forward his work.

Second, the outpouring of the Holy Spirit at Pentecost could have happened only to that particular group. Why? They had known Jesus intimately from beginning to end of his ministry. They shared a holy memory of what Jesus said and did. They had witnessed the risen Lord from time to time. Through what Jesus had taught and through their own understanding of Scripture (the Old Testament), they were already well on the way to beholding Jesus as the Christ, the Messiah. Finally, they were present when Jesus promised the Holy Spirit and commissioned them to be his witnesses.

Third, just as Jesus had foretold, the Holy Spirit acted at Pentecost to glorify Jesus as Lord and Savior. What Jesus had said about the Holy Spirit in relation to himself was confirmed by the events of Pentecost. This is presupposed in the outpouring upon that particular group. It is seen in the fact that the outpouring consisted in no small degree in the illuminating, communicating, teaching power of the "Spirit of truth." As a result, those earliest Christians knew—not merely with their minds but with their total beings—the glory of God in Jesus Christ.

Fourth, out of this magnificent divine revelation came the absolute *commitment* that characterized those Christians after Pentecost. They began immediately to carry out the commission of their risen Lord. They were concerned, as Jesus had been, for the poor and needy. They had a passion for souls which was connected with their desire to bring liberation to persons oppressed and in captivity.

Fifth, the Holy Spirit formed those followers of Jesus into a believing, worshiping, praying, and serving *community* of faith. In a true sense, the Holy Spirit created the church at Pentecost. And its one foundation was and is and shall be Jesus Christ her Lord.

What Paul Said

One more primary authoritative source in the New Testament needs to be considered. I refer to certain judicious utterances and to the inspired example of the apostle Paul. Here no single passage will do. We need to look at a few selected passages from Paul's letters and also at certain emphases in his teachings and in his life as a Christian leader.

• Paul had a genius for going to the point. In writing to the Christians at Corinth he said, "No one can say 'Jesus is Lord' except by the Holy Spirit." (1 Corinthians 12:3) The words, "Jesus is Lord," formed one of the earliest confessions of faith. Paul was reminding the Corinthian Christians that no one can really say those words without the assistance of the Holy Spirit. Here, again, in keeping with two other great passages we have discussed (John 16:7-15; Acts 2), Paul insisted that the Holy Spirit links us directly with Jesus Christ as Lord.

Paul came very close to identifying the Holy Spirit with the spirit of the risen Christ. He said, "Now the Lord is the Spirit, and where the Spirit of the Lord is, there is freedom. And we all, with unveiled face, beholding the glory of the Lord, are being changed into his likeness from one degree of glory to another; for this comes from the Lord who is the Spirit." (2 Corinthians 3:17-18)

Beyond question Paul made it impossible to separate the work of the Holy Spirit from that of Jesus Christ as Lord and Redeemer. At the same time, in order to deal with certain special problems of divisiveness among the Corinthians, Paul shared with them some practical implications of the Holy Spirit's work.

● Paul wrote more about his own interpretation of Christianity than did any other writer of the New Testament. In addition to his explicit statements, already mentioned, his words often *imply* thoughts on the Holy Spirit. His deepdown convictions on the Holy Spirit are reflected in his personal testimony as to what Christ meant to him and in his emphasis on a Spirit-filled life.

Paul was an authoritative example of how a Christian leader performs when he is filled with the Holy Spirit. His life teaches us as much as his explicit remarks on the Spirit. Through his ministry as a whole, Paul gives us a kind of confirmation of the work of the Holy Spirit in a gifted human being totally dedicated to Jesus Christ. We see in Paul what happens when the Holy Spirit re-creates a person to carry forward the Lord's work in the world.

From Paul's life and teachings, then, what are we to say about the Holy Spirit? I suggest one magnificent theme that brings together everything he said. This theme expresses or implies the directives, already discussed, which Jesus himself gave. It confirms also the authenticity, the genuineness, of the great outpouring at Pentecost.

Paul's Great Theme
● The centrality and finality of Jesus Christ as the Savior of the world was Paul's theme. To him this was intimately personal. Jesus Christ was the basic reality of his existence as a Christian. So he said, "For to me to live is Christ, and to die is gain." (Philippians 1:21) And again, "I have been crucified with Christ; it is no longer I who live, but Christ who lives in me; and the life I now live in the flesh I live by faith in the Son of God, who loved me and gave himself for me." (Galatians 2:20)

The number of Paul's references to Jesus Christ as Redeemer and Lord overwhelms the reader of his letters. For him everything depends on Jesus' life, death, and resurrection. Some people think of their own Christian experiences as the final ground of belief. Not so Paul. He knew the presence of the living Christ in his soul, but he proclaimed only the authority and finality of Jesus Christ crucified and raised from the dead. This reality, confirmed in experience, stands in its own right in the far-reaching providence of God. Paul never allowed his Christian experience to obscure the risen Lord who gave it to him.

● The gospel is the good news of Jesus Christ. "For I delivered to you as of first importance," said Paul, "what I also received, that Christ died for our sins in accordance with the scriptures . . ." (1 Corinthians 15:3) Then Paul went on to speak of Jesus' resurrection and of his appearances to the disciples and others, including Paul himself. (15:4-8) Though unworthy because he had persecuted the church, he was what he was by the grace of God. (15:9-10)

According to Paul, God made possible the new era of salvation by grace through Jesus Christ. He experienced this himself, but he proclaimed it as God's gift to all who would repent and have faith. In one of his finest and therefore most familiar passages he said, "There is therefore now no condemnation for those who are in Christ Jesus. For the law of the Spirit of life in Christ Jesus has set me free from the law of sin and death. For God has done what the law, weakened by the flesh, could not do: sending his own Son in the likeness of sinful flesh and for sin, he condemned sin in the flesh, in order that the just requirement of the law might be fulfilled in us, who walk not according to the flesh but according to the Spirit." (Romans 8:1-4)

Paul wrote to the Christians at Rome, "But you are not in the flesh, you are in the Spirit, if in fact the Spirit of God dwells in you. Any one who does not have the Spirit of Christ does not belong to him." (Romans 8:9)

● The illuminating presence of the Spirit is seen in Paul's persistent interpretation of Scripture (the Old Testament) as preparatory to the coming of Jesus Christ, the promised Messiah. Of course, this was the characteristic approach of all the earliest Christian leaders, from Peter (Acts 2:25-28, 34, 39), to Stephen (Chapter 7), to Philip (8:26-35), and others. Paul made it a special point at the great city of Antioch, as well as at the other cities where he worked, to teach on the basis of Scripture that Jesus was the Christ.

The Spirit of truth was illuminating his understanding to assist him in interpreting Scripture.

● Through the Holy Spirit the Christians were bound to one another as members of the body of Christ. The Holy Spirit filled Paul with the passion to create local churches. Just as the Spirit formed the church at Pentecost, so the Spirit continued his concern to keep the gospel alive through Paul's determination to form and nurture local churches wherever he went. The letters to the various churches (at Corinth, Ephesus, Philippi, Thessalonica, Rome, and in Galatia) illustrate this. And, as we have seen, the Holy Spirit magnifies Jesus Christ by bringing people together in the unity of the Spirit.

Paul's desire for unity in the church at Corinth is seen in 1 Corinthians 12 through 14. The church was divided over leadership and over spiritual gifts. Paul likened the Christians there to the various parts of a human body. (12:12-31) "For just as the body is one and has many members, and all the members of the body, though many, are one body, so it is with Christ. For by one Spirit we were all baptized into one body—Jews or Greeks, slave or free—and all were made to drink of one Spirit." (12:12-13)

Then, for the first time in writing, Paul said, "Now you are the body of Christ." (12:27)

Gifts of the Spirit

A word about Paul's understanding of the gifts of the Spirit needs to be added against this background. Paul understood all special gifts of the Spirit as means of carrying forward the mission of Jesus Christ in the churches and in the world. The varieties of gifts were, like the various parts of the body, designed to benefit the whole community of faith, for we have one Spirit, one Lord, and one baptism. (1 Corinthians 12:4-13)

After listing various specialized gifts of the Spirit, Paul pleaded with the Christians at Corinth to desire earnestly "the higher gifts." (12:31) He said, "Make love your aim, and earnestly desire the spiritual gifts" (14:1), for these gifts produce the fruit of the Spirit: "love, joy, peace, patience, kindness, goodness, faithfulness, gentleness, self-control." (Galatians 5:22-23) The Spirit gives the Christlike spirit.

THE HOLY SPIRIT
AND THE CHURCH

4

The Holy Spirit and the Historic Community Of Faith

The crossed keys in this symbol for Peter refer to Matthew 16:19. The inverted cross comes from the legend that Peter felt unworthy to die in the same manner as his Lord and asked to be crucified head downward.

We have observed that Jesus was concerned to send the Holy Spirit upon his followers who were united in their common commitment. We have seen that at Pentecost the Holy Spirit brought together Jesus' followers into a dynamic fellowship and filled them all with new resources for creative living. We have noted also that, according to Paul, the Holy Spirit is specially at work to re-create and nurture people within the community of faith.

Therefore, just as it is impossible to separate the mission of the Holy Spirit from Jesus Christ, so is it out of the question to separate the mission of the Holy Spirit from the Christian community of faith. Only in and through the church that bears his name has Jesus Christ been proclaimed and experienced as Lord and Redeemer from generation to generation. The point is that the power of the Holy Spirit has been at work to form people into communities of faith in Jesus Christ. And the Holy Spirit has strengthened them in their common life and witness.

● The community of faith—every local church—has been especially precious in the sight of God. The Holy Spirit has been uniquely and distinctively at work whenever people have been gathered together in Jesus' name. But if the Holy Spirit has had this special affinity for the historic community of faith, he has been necessarily concerned to act in ways that not only created the church but also re-created, nurtured, and expanded it.

The Spirit at Work in the Church

To be specific, the Holy Spirit has worked in and through the historic community of faith to fulfill five purposes of utmost importance: (1) the preservation of the identity and integrity of the gospel; (2) the calling of ministers to proclaim the gospel, to teach the Word, and to administer the sacraments; (3) the summons of all Christians to responsible living in community; (4) the baptism of persons, and the formation of Jesus' followers into supportive communities of faith; and (5) the evangelization of the world.

This is an oversimplified statement, for in each of these areas of activity the Holy Spirit has worked under difficulties since the days of the early church. Human pride, prejudice, imbalance, corruption, and even crankiness have entered into the life of the church since the earliest days. Even Peter and Paul had to deal with these problems.

Consider the pangs of Christian concern which Paul felt when he wrote: "O foolish Galatians! Who has bewitched you, before whose eyes Jesus Christ was publicly portrayed as crucified? Let me ask you only this: Did you receive the Spirit by works of the law, or by hearing with faith? Are you so foolish? Having begun with the Spirit, are you now ending with the flesh?" (Galatians 3:1-3)

We may ask, Why couldn't the Holy Spirit overrule the errors, distortions, and corruptions of the gospel and the Christian life?

The answer is that, despite the ignorance, folly, pride, and prejudice of people, the Holy Spirit does not force his way into their minds and hearts. He confronts, persuades, and woos but does not tyrannize them. There has always been a struggle to maintain the integrity of the gospel.

There has always been a struggle to confront gifted and dedicated people with the call to the ministry. In every era there has been the struggle for justice and human welfare. Incorporating people into a dynamic body of believers (baptism and its implications) has always been a difficult task. And there has always been the struggle to evangelize. Nevertheless, in *these five great areas of the church's need and work* the Holy Spirit has acted to bless the ongoing community of faith. How so? Let us take a closer look at the presence of the Holy Spirit in all five of these areas.

The Integrity of the Gospel

How has the power of the Holy Spirit been at work in the church to preserve the integrity of the gospel? Primarily through Scripture, creed, sacrament, hymn, orderly worship, theological debate, and new visitations from God.

Paul saw how easily the minds of people were swayed. We read, "so that we may no longer be children, tossed to and fro and carried about with every wind of doctrine, by the cunning of men, by their craftiness in deceitful wiles." (Ephesians 4:14) The plain fact is that it has always been unbelievable what people will believe. Where religion is concerned, people have always needed a single basic guide. Hence, the importance of the Bible, of revealed religion with its confirmation in experience and in the fruits of the Spirit.

The church has never been able to evangelize by proclaiming human discoveries. Her life and power have been seen in proclaiming *God's* good news in Christ. And this is no human discovery: it is a divine revelation. When we reflect on the numberless ideas people have picked up through the centuries, and when we consider the strife of systems, the clashes among ideologies, and the vast oceans of prejudices, follies, superstitions, and even the errors by gifted minds in the church itself—when we think on these things, it seems like a miracle of divine grace that the church has been able to maintain the essential integrity of the gospel for these two thousand years.

● How has it been possible? Primarily because the Holy Spirit has been at work in the historic community of faith in the creation of the *authoritative sacred writings* of the

Bible. Only in this way has it been possible to preach and teach the revealed story of God's gracious love in Jesus Christ. The Bible is the church's book; it is the church's indispensable guide.

We cannot put into words easily how much the Bible has meant both to the church and to Western civilization. But this much is sure: It has given essential unity to Christian people. It has given them a revealed world view with God as the only ultimate reality. It has conveyed the fact of the Father's love and presence in the world. It has made known and kept alive the marvelous story of the divine initiative in Jesus Christ. And it has kept the community of faith aware of the vast resources of God's grace.

The close link between the Holy Spirit and the Bible did not occur by accident. From the beginning Christians have believed that the writers of the sacred scriptures were inspired by the Holy Spirit. This is not to say that the writers themselves played no creative role in the process, for their thoughts entered into the revelations through the Holy Spirit. God has revealed himself through people, in earthly settings, and in historical events. The initiative of the Holy Spirit was no less real because people were involved in the process. The main point is that the Holy Spirit has acted to reveal God's nature through persons.

Most of Paul's letters, for example, were written to meet specific needs of churches that he had founded or in which he had labored. They were not written to be parts of the New Testament. As Christians read these letters, they realized that they were of God. Under the inspiration of the Holy Spirit, Paul had written. And under the same inspiration of the Holy Spirit the church had selected his writings—and discarded others—for inclusion in what we call the New Testament.

In this manner, then, the continuing body of believers came to have an authoritative guide for Christian belief and practice.

The Holy Spirit has assisted all who turned to the Bible seriously to understand it aright. The Holy Spirit has witnessed in the hearts of Christians of every era to confirm the genuineness of the biblical revelation. The confirmation has not taken place in the hearts of isolated Christians.

Rather, it has occurred as they participated in the life of the historic community of faith.

● The church has always known that the Bible must be understood and interpreted rightly. In every era differences of interpretation have occurred, but in basic beliefs there has been extensive agreement. The Holy Spirit has helped Christians understand the vast movement of divine revelation as beginning in creation, continuing through Moses, David, and the prophets, and coming to fulfillment in Jesus Christ.

The Holy Spirit has helped Christians understand the Bible as God's Word for man's response. It was never a dead book. It was the *living* Word—the Father forever wooing, communicating, striving, caring, drawing people into the orbit of his love.

Great verses of the Bible have been instruments of the Holy Spirit probing the depths of our human nature. The Holy Spirit has used the story of Jesus in mysterious ways to enable people to see the dimensions of their sin and folly and to draw them to the Savior.

The Holy Spirit has used the promises of the Bible to put hope in the place of despair, to help men respond gratefully to God's power to forgive and save to the uttermost. The glory of the sacred book is that the Spirit has used it to transform the lives of persons for constructive service.

● The Holy Spirit has been at work also to preserve the integrity of the gospel through creed, symbol, hymn, and sacrament. These and other elements of the great Christian tradition have been formed and nurtured with the aid of the Holy Spirit. They summarize and support the biblical revelation.

For example, the integrity of the gospel is clearly retained in the sacrament of the Lord's Supper. Jesus began this by commanding his followers to eat the bread in memory of his broken body and to drink from the cup in memory of his shed blood. (Matthew 26:26-29; 1 Corinthians 11:23-26) The Holy Spirit has enabled the historic community of faith to grasp something of the depths and riches of God's love in the death of Jesus Christ for the redemption of the world.

The symbol of the cross has been at the heart of the

church's centers of worship from earliest times. It is a perpetual reminder of the integrity of the gospel of salvation in Jesus Christ. Here again the Holy Spirit has helped worshipers experience something of the mystery of God's mighty action in Jesus Christ.

The Spirit and the Ordained Ministry

The unique presence of the Holy Spirit in the community of faith is seen also in the ordained ministry. Jesus called the twelve apostles. He assigned them to positions of leadership in the continuing community of faith. When Judas betrayed Jesus and killed himself, he was replaced by Matthias who "was enrolled with the eleven apostles." (Acts 1:26)

Note how Matthias came to be chosen: He had to meet at least one condition. Luke quotes Peter as saying that the one chosen must have been with the disciples "during all the time that the Lord Jesus went in and out among us, beginning from the baptism of John until the day when he was taken up from us . . . must become with us a witness to his resurrection." (Acts 1:21-22)

In other words, Jesus acted to set aside leaders for the work of the Kingdom. *He* established the principle of a called ministry. Those apostles were in the specially privileged position of being witnesses of Jesus' life, death, and resurrection. Therefore, they supplied the directives for Christian ministers of all succeeding generations.

● The idea of a succession in the ministry going back to the apostles has profound meaning. It should not be understood primarily in terms of an unbroken line, from the apostles to the present day, of persons ordained by the laying on of hands. Rather, *we have the apostolic succession through the Holy Spirit* of a ministry in the continuing community of faith, beginning with Jesus and the apostles. The Holy Spirit has called people to proclaim the gospel. He set them apart for the ministry of Word, sacrament, and service.

We can see that unless some persons are called of God and set apart through the church for the ministry, Christ's work will not be carried forward effectively. Paul knew this when he said, "But how are men to call upon him in whom

According to tradition Barnabas was a great preacher who was stoned to death, symbolized by the open Bible and the stones.

they have not believed? And how are they to believe in him of whom they have never heard? And how are they to hear without a preacher? And how can men preach unless they are sent? As it is written, 'How beautiful are the feet of those who preach good news!'" (Romans 10:14-15) Paul knew this in an intimately personal way when he said of his own ministry, "I am entrusted with a commission." (1 Corinthians 9:17) Where would the early church have been without Paul and his call to the ministry?

The Holy Spirit has always been concerned for the called and ordained ministry. He has confronted persons with the meaning and challenge of the ministry. Just as he called Paul, Augustine, Luther, Calvin, Wesley, Albright, and Otterbein, so he continues to call persons to devote themselves wholly to the work of the ministry.

This does not mean that the Holy Spirit has called persons in any one way only. Some have received an extraordinary call. They could never doubt that great moment when they knew that God had summoned them for a life commitment to the ordained ministry. The call of Saul of Tarsus was like that. But others were called by the Holy Spirit through more gradual processes.

● Are there signs of the call to the ministry? Have these become evident during the long centuries of Christian history? They have. The Holy Spirit has called persons when, in their highest and holiest moments, they felt the recurring sense that God wanted them for his special work of preaching, teaching, administering the sacraments, and leading in Jesus Christ's work of compassion and justice.

The Spirit has called when men and women were given

the vision to see that the deepest needs of people could be met only through Jesus Christ and his church.

The Spirit has called through the compassion for people which has burned like a divine flame in the hearts of persons open to the will of God.

The Spirit has called through dedicated ministers whose example and teaching gave young people a new vision of what God might do through them.

The Spirit has called young people through the experience of participating in the life of the church and in the consequent awareness that this was their divinely appointed life work.

The Spirit has called persons to the ordained ministry through extensive negative experiences of life—frustration, boredom, meaninglessness, guilt, anxiety, despair—in which they began to behold by contrast something of the unutterable glory of God's good news in Jesus Christ.

The Spirit has called people to the ministry through those numberless local churches where faith was born and nurtured, where dedicated people—fathers, mothers, lay persons—suggested, guided, hoped, and prayed to the end that the call might be heard.

Every authentic minister in every era of the church could have told his own story here. Each story would have its unique and intimately personal dimensions. But throughout there would be the one mighty mysterious fact: the awesome reality that the Holy Spirit had called by his mysterious power in and through the community of faith. A second attending fact would be that the community of faith had recognized the call and authorized the ordination of those called. In and through each experience would be the sense of awe, of inadequacy, of the desire to do one's best for the Lord, of the passion for souls, of concern for the well-being of people, and of the ever recurring need for prayer and divine grace.

The Call to Responsible Living

The presence of the Holy Spirit in the church has been manifested in the summons to responsible living in community. Christians are not isolated from the world in which they live, and the Spirit strives to enable them to reflect Christ's love in their deeds. More will be said on this in a later chapter. Here let it be noted that the Holy Spirit is present not only in life's mountaintop experiences but also in the daily rounds of love and duty. The Spirit sustains and empowers people in the workaday realms where responsible living takes place.

The Spirit and Baptism

The Holy Spirit is especially at work in the sacrament of baptism.

Our risen Lord gave three commands to his followers which have been of utmost importance throughout Christian history. He said, "stay," "go," and "baptize." The disciples were commanded to stay in Jerusalem until "clothed with power from on high." (Luke 24:49; see also Acts 1:4-8.) The risen Lord commanded them also to "go . . . and make disciples of all nations" (Matthew 28:19) and to be his witnesses wherever there are human beings (Acts 1:8).

The significance of our risen Lord's command to baptize is often overlooked. He said, Baptize people "in the name of the Father and of the Son and of the Holy Spirit." (Matthew 28:19) Baptism is the *sacrament of incorporation* into the community of faith. It is no mere act of purification. Rather, it is a specific act or ceremony that implies the whole life of the church in her many acts of teaching and Christian nurture. (28:20) Our Lord knew that there could be no sustained vital religion apart from community. He commanded the disciples to bring people into the corporate fellowship of believers wherein they could grow and work together for their common lord. Baptism is, therefore, specially connected with the work of the Holy Spirit.

The Power to Witness

The Holy Spirit's dynamic presence in the community of faith has also been seen in the yearning to evangelize the world.

● The most amazing evidence of the activity of the Holy Spirit following that first Pentecost was the power of those Christians to witness effectively. Thousands were converted. (Acts 2:41; 4:4; 5:14; 6:7). To be sure, many of these thousands had had some previous contact with Jesus. They had heard him preach and teach. They were present when he performed miracles. Indeed, some of them had

been healed by him. They were also aware of the Crucifixion. In addition, those who were filled with the Holy
Spirit at Pentecost had recently been with their risen Lord.
The event of the Resurrection filled their minds with a
sense of the wonder, mystery, and glory of God's mighty
action in behalf of men. The Holy Spirit turned the holy
remembrance of these events, so fresh on their minds, into a
dynamic source of witness. They witnessed to the glory of
God in Jesus Christ with special emphasis on the Resurrection.

This power from the Holy Spirit to witness was seen not
only around Jerusalem but also at Antioch and elsewhere.
For example, the Holy Spirit enabled certain Christian laymen from Cyprus and Cyrene to witness with power at
Antioch and "a great number that believed turned to the
Lord." (Acts 11:20-21) Then, when Barnabas, "a good man,
full of the Holy Spirit and of faith," was sent there from
Jerusalem, "a large company was added to the Lord." (Acts
11:22-24) Barnabas, needing help, went to Tarsus and
brought Saul back to Antioch (one of the three largest
cities of the Roman Empire). And here is what Luke wrote:
"For a whole year they met with the church, and taught
a large company of people; and in Antioch the disciples
were for the first time called Christians." (11:26)

● What was the source of this extraordinary power to
witness? The Holy Spirit. Put it this way: Through the
power of the Holy Spirit those early Christians at Jerusalem,
Antioch, and elsewhere beheld the glory of what God had
done in Jesus Christ. They recovered the vision of God's
dealings with Moses and the prophets in the past as recorded in the only scriptures they had (what we call the
Old Testament). They experienced the holy memory of
Jesus' life, death, and resurrection. Through the Spirit they
were given a holy awareness of the individual's desperate
need for God's salvation. They saw people as creatures
lost in the shadowy realms of sin, ineffectiveness, futility,
and death.

These early Christians experienced the new life in Christ,
the new principle of inner power and righteousness by
grace through faith. It was the power of the Holy Spirit.
Also they were given the vision of God's plan to carry forward the work of the Kingdom through Jesus Christ. As

written in Ephesians, "For he [God] has made known to us in all wisdom and insight the mystery of his will, according to his purpose which he set forth in Christ as a plan for the fulness of time, to unite all things in him, things in heaven and things on earth." (1:9-10)

In short, the evangelistic power of those earliest Christians was no accident. Nor was it "cooked up." This power was not engendered by conventions and programs—though these have their rightful places. It came from tarrying in Jerusalem under the immediate glow of the holy vision of God's preparatory work in the prophets. It came from the vision of God's great salvation in Jesus Christ. And it came from God's presence through the Holy Spirit in the heart. These early Christians knew the wonder and mystery of *revealed* religion. They *experienced* the power that comes only from an openness and absolute commitment to Jesus Christ. They *had* to witness. They were compelled, by the power of the Spirit, to tell what God had done.

This was what moved the Christians at Antioch to send Paul and Barnabas on that first missionary journey. (Acts 13:1 through 15:35) This is what moved Paul to go to Macedonia, to Philippi, Thessalonica, Berea, on down to Athens and Corinth, and over to Ephesus. (Acts 16:6 through 18:21) The Holy Spirit's presence as an evangelistic passion is seen in Paul's sense of compulsion. As he said, "For if I preach the gospel, that gives me no ground for boasting. For necessity is laid upon me. Woe to me if I do not preach the gospel!" (1 Corinthians 9:16)

Many Christians throughout the centuries have been set in motion by this same desire to communicate the gospel wherever they could. They have heard again and again the promise of their risen Lord: "But you shall receive power when the Holy Spirit has come upon you; and you shall be my witnesses in Jerusalem and in all Judea and Samaria and to the end of the earth." (Acts 1:8) They have heard their Lord's command: "Go therefore and make disciples of all nations, baptizing them in the name of the Father and of the Son and of the Holy Spirit." (Matthew 28:19)

Sometimes the Holy Spirit gave people the power to witness through the formation of new local churches or societies. Sometimes this power led to the creation of schools, monasteries, hospitals, homes, and social agencies. But always the one supreme objective was bringing people together in Jesus Christ and in his church.

● We should remember, however, that the power to witness did not always bring those overwhelming responses referred to in the earlier parts of the Book of Acts. Often there was violent opposition. Christians were persecuted. Paul's career illustrates this. In spite of his great successes as a missionary, he still suffered at the hands of the enemies of Christ. (2 Corinthians 11:24-29)

The evangelical mission of Christianity has never been easy. Jesus did not promise an easy time for his followers, but he did promise them the sustaining and empowering presence of the Spirit. The blood of the martyrs has indeed been the seed of the church.

Augustine was keenly aware of the difficulties. And he may be allowed here to represent thousands of others. He spoke of striving for souls as "a mighty load, grievous toil." And so it has always been. For this reason many in all centuries have taken refuge in the easier ways. Many also worked hard and shared in the "grievous toil." The ongoing church of Jesus Christ bears magnificent testimony to their evangelistic activity.

John Wesley has to be listed among those who followed in the line of men and women who through the Holy Spirit were given the power to witness effectively. Though many others, such as Philip Otterbein and Jacob Albright, should be studied in a more comprehensive report, Wesley and his followers may be mentioned as among the most notable examples of evangelical religion in the Christian heritage.

5

The Holy Spirit and The Wesleyan Heritage

The medallion showing the dove of peace encircled by the serpent of healing was used extensively by Wesley in City Road Chapel, London.

We have seen that the Holy Spirit has manifested himself across the centuries by creating and nurturing the church. Now we are to consider the movement of the Holy Spirit in a particular grouping of Christians, namely, those in the United Methodist heritage.

Here the primary guide is John Wesley, who set the tone for United Methodism's emphasis on the Holy Spirit. He guided his followers into the particular understanding of the Holy Spirit that has always been characteristic of this heritage at its best. While John Wesley will be the primary figure in this discussion, we have in mind also Asbury, Albright, Otterbein, and many others who shared deeply in his interest in the work of the Holy Spirit.

• Wesley was guided by Scripture, and particularly by Jesus and the apostles. On this basis he believed that the infinite God of the universe has chosen to make his vast resources available to persons through the presence and power of the Holy Spirit. Wesley was fascinated by the *availability in experience* of the dynamic power of God. He knew this to be the central feature of apostolic religion. He interpreted Jesus' promise of the Holy Spirit in this way, and he viewed Paul's teaching in this light.

In his brief comments on Paul's words on the law of the Spirit and related matters, Wesley emphasized, as Paul did, the sway of the Holy Spirit over our lives. Those who walk not after the flesh but after the Spirit (Romans 8:5) are guided in thought, word, and deed by the Spirit of God. Those "in the Spirit" (8:9) are "under his government." And those "led by the Spirit of God" (8:14) are "in all the ways of righteousness." [1]

Persons who have made a careful study of John Wesley's aims know of his untiring emphasis on the work of the Holy Spirit in regeneration and sanctification. The same could be said of Charles Wesley. The Methodist movement was from the beginning a call to recover apostolic Christianity by the power of the Holy Spirit.

● In contrast to a barren ceremonialism, to a fruitless legalism, to an austere predestinarianism, to a degrading antinomianism (disregard of God's commandments and of morality), to a mystical quietism, and to a cold intellectualism, Wesley championed *vitally experienced religion.* He felt compelled to proclaim the Holy Spirit's power to transform fallen people into new creations and to set them on their way toward holy living.

In designing City Road Chapel in London, John Wesley used the symbol of the encircled dove repeatedly around the front of the entire gallery. Sermon, prayer, hymn, class meeting, and Christian living were permeated with the assumption of the presence and power of the Holy Spirit. This apostolic affirmation of the life-changing, continuing activity of the Holy Spirit was a primary characteristic of the Wesleyan movement.

● We need to bear in mind, however, that in this heritage the stress on the Holy Spirit *had certain characteristic features.* A brief look at these is essential to a true understanding of the Holy Spirit in the Wesleyan heritage. To

---

[1] *Explanatory Notes Upon the New Testament,* by John Wesley.

be specific, John Wesley's emphasis on the Holy Spirit had at least four distinctive features.

"The Whole of Real Religion"

First, the work of the Holy Spirit was understood by Wesley in the context of the *whole sweep of revealed religion.* The biblical revelation of God as Creator, Redeemer, and Holy Spirit was always kept intact, with never any danger of lapsing into a unitarianism of the Spirit.

Some people so emphasize the activity of the Holy Spirit that they tend to forget about the Father and the Son. A primary error of sect-type thought is that it tends to take an *aspect* of Christian truth and make it either the center or the whole of it.

John Wesley viewed the activity of the Holy Spirit as expressing the revealed purpose of God in Christ to remake the lives of all people and to sustain them for righteous living. The Holy Spirit's work is not only with the new birth but with "the whole of real religion." [2]

Every Stage of Christian Experience

Second, on the basis of Scripture Wesley taught that the Holy Spirit is present and active in *every major stage of Christian experience.* With him the Spirit's activity is related to personal experiences. A religion that is not experienced is dead and fruitless. A religion that does not help us identify wherein the Holy Spirit is at work in us leaves much to be desired. Wesley taught that the Holy Spirit's activity needs to be identified in the stages leading toward righteous living through faith in Jesus Christ— God is concerned with an inner transformation that leads directly into deeds of love and mercy.

Observe that we are dealing here with Wesley's understanding of the *primary* and *indispensable* stages in the formation of the Christian life. He believed that, in unusual instances, the Holy Spirit might act to make people speak in unknown tongues or to cure diseases or to perform miracles; but he never emphasized these as essentials in Christian experience and life.

● One mark of Wesley's genius was that in stressing the

---

[2] *The Letters of John Wesley,* IV, 339.

work of the Holy Spirit, he, like Paul, did not lapse into the idea that the Holy Spirit's primary mission was to lead people to do odd and spectacular acts—acts not available to or desired by all men who seek salvation. According to Wesley, the Holy Spirit is initially *present in every human being prior to his conscious acceptance of Jesus Christ* as Redeemer and Lord. No one is without the activity of the Holy Spirit on this preliminary level. This was called *prevenient grace*—the grace or the presence of the Holy Spirit that precedes the grace that comes with the acceptance of Jesus Christ as Lord.

Wesley believed that human nature, in its unredeemed or natural state, is sinful. It is infected with a radical evil. This condition is incurable apart from divine grace. For this reason people cannot be filled with righteous impulses unless they are redeemed and empowered with the Holy Spirit. But, if persons are thus "naturally inclined toward evil and that continuously," how is it possible for them to turn to God at all?

Calvin answered this question by saying that some are simply *elected* by God for salvation and others are not. Wesley answered the question by saying that the Holy Spirit is at work in *all human beings* to help them open their souls to God. Salvation is not for the chosen few but for everyone. This is possible because the Holy Spirit is at work on this preparatory level (prevenient grace) in *all* human beings.

● The Holy Spirit is present also in enabling people to have faith in God's forgiving love in Jesus Christ. That is, the Holy Spirit acts in people to enable them to experience the new birth or conversion.

Here we may note wherein Wesley agreed with and differed from Luther. You will recall that Luther made the biblical doctrine of justification by faith the pivot on which all his theology revolved. Wesley agreed precisely with Luther regarding justification (forgiveness) by God's graciousness in Christ through faith and not by our works. He was as clear on that as Luther was.[3] The efforts by

---

[3] William R. Cannon has treated this topic in his work, *The Theology of John Wesley* (Abingdon Press, 1946); see pp. 145-50, 222-25. Out of print.

some to minimize the distinction between Wesley and Luther on this—a distinction Wesley insisted upon—are largely misguided.

Wesley understood justification or the new birth as the beginning of sanctification (inner holiness). That is, the Holy Spirit's work of righteousness was already made real in us here and now. Luther said that righteousness in the Christian is only a hope to be realized after death. In this present life the Christian has only an imputed righteousness; that is, one is regarded as righteous merely because of Christ. Wesley, on the contrary, taught that though one may be far from perfect, he is *now being made righteous* through the power of the Holy Spirit.

The new birth, in Wesley's view, is preparatory to sanctification (inner holiness). The Holy Spirit is present in the total process of Christian growth, for, as we have seen, God's primary concern is to assist persons in the inward righteousness that expresses itself in deeds of love and mercy. The divine summons to Christian growth has no end. The Holy Spirit is constantly active in the redeemed to perfect them in love and wisdom.

● Wesley believed that the Holy Spirit wanted people to experience *a more advanced work of grace* whereby they would be cleansed from inner corruption and *made perfect in their intention* to express Christ's love in thought, word, and deed. But he never professed this experience himself.

This teaching was his way of emphasizing *the continuing boundless resources of the Spirit* for re-creating the inner souls of persons for righteous living. We would be making a fundamental error to suppose that Wesley would ever restrict the activity of the Holy Spirit to two definite works of grace—conversion and sanctification or inner holiness. He clearly and emphatically urged his followers to seek the re-creative power of the Holy Spirit which goes beyond the new birth and which is available increasingly to every Christian.

Wesley added nothing new to the doctrinal understanding of the Holy Spirit. But he rendered a distinctive service to vital Christianity by insisting on the concrete differences made in the hearts of persons by the sanctifying work of the Holy Spirit. That is, the Holy Spirit is God dynamically present for good at every stage of Christian experience and especially is he present in the quest for perfection in love.

Persons in the Wesleyan heritage have differed over whether the Holy Spirit completely eradicated man's depraved nature or repressed it. They have debated over whether the sanctifying action of the Spirit was instantaneous or gradual. They have agreed, however, that the new birth is the start of the new life that is to unfold toward perfection. Justification, conversion, the new birth —this is the grand beginning that calls for the continuing thrust of the Holy Spirit's movement in sanctification.

● Writing on justification (forgiveness) and sanctification (inner holiness), Wesley complained that many persons have been confused on how these are related to each other. Luther, he said, wrote clearly on justification but knew almost nothing of sanctification. Certain Roman Catholics knew a lot about sanctification but were not clear on justification.

Wesley said: "But it has pleased God to give the Methodists a full and clear knowledge of each, and the wide difference between them.

"They know, indeed, that at the same time a man is justified, sanctification properly begins. For when he is justified, he is 'born again,' 'born of the Spirit'; which, although it is not (as some suppose) the whole process of sanctification, is doubtless the gate of it. Of this, likewise, God has given them a full view. . . .

"And as, in the natural birth, a man is born at once, and then grows larger and stronger by degrees; so in the spiritual birth, a man is born at once, and then gradually increases in spiritual stature and strength. The new birth, therefore, is the first point of sanctification, which may increase more and more unto the perfect day.

". . . They [Methodists] know God has joined these together, and it is not for man to put them asunder: Therefore they maintain, with equal zeal and diligence, the doctrine of free, full, present justification, on the one hand, and of entire sanctification both of heart and life, on the other; being as tenacious of inward holiness as any Mystic, and of outward, as any Pharisee."[4]

---

[4] *The Works of John Wesley,* Sermon CVll, "On God's Vineyard," part I, sections 5-8.

Harald Lindstrom has summarized this by saying that "the essence and prime end of Methodism is sanctity, or the moral transformation of the heart and life of man." [5] Eric Baker has brought this theme to clear focus in *The Faith of a Methodist*. There he says that the unique emphasis in Methodism lies chiefly ". . . in the stress continually placed by Wesley on the Doctrine of Christian Perfection."[6] This, of course, has nothing to do with a human achievement but with the boundless open-ended activity of the Holy Spirit toward perfection in love.

Tests for Genuine Christian Experience

A third characteristic feature of Wesley's emphasis on the Holy Spirit is his practical tests for the authenticity, or genuineness, of Christian experiences. He was constantly aware of those spiritual leaders and groups who tended toward fanaticism, or, to use his term, "enthusiasm." So he taught his followers to test their claims by their conduct. Jesus said that everyone can recognize false prophets by their fruits. "Are grapes gathered from thorns, or figs from thistles? So, every sound tree bears good fruit, but the bad tree bears evil fruit." (Matthew 7:16-17)

Wesley gave much attention to this idea. No matter what claims people might make about visions, revelations, tongues, new experiences, prophetic powers, and the like, Wesley always came back to the two basic guides: *the plain teaching of Scripture* and *the clear evidences of conduct*.

During his day, as in all eras, whenever Christians have stressed the Holy Spirit, the attending dangers of fanaticism and untested claims existed. Some persons witnessed to visions; others claimed direct illuminations leading them to despise Bible study, public worship, the sacraments, sermon preparation, and other means of grace. Still others affirmed the power to heal or the gift of tongues.

Wesley believed in these as special gifts made available particularly during the days of the apostles and rarely afterward. He never led his followers to suppose that the primary work of the Holy Spirit was these spectacular acts.

---

[5] From *Wesley and Sanctification*, by Harald Lindstrom (Epworth Press, 1946), p. 103. Out of print.

[6] From *The Faith of a Methodist*, by Eric Baker (Abingdon Press, 1959), p. 21.

Why? Because he believed that the God of the Bible is primarily interested in the practical good living of his children and in winning people to Jesus Christ. In the Wesleyan heritage, then, the emphasis is upon love and on what Paul referred to as "the higher gifts" of the Spirit. (1 Corinthians 12:31)

In the end Wesley wanted his followers to ask themselves two searching questions about any of their claims to an unusual experience of the Holy Spirit. First, does this experience help us grow as Christians? Second, does it make us more effective in serving others? If the answer is Yes to both questions, the Holy Spirit is manifestly at work in and through us. If not, we deceive ourselves. So the test is not the *claims* to the presence and power of the Holy Spirit but the scriptural guideline of judging by the "fruits" of the Spirit in our lives.

Moral Conduct

A fourth characteristic feature of Wesley's emphasis on the Holy Spirit is closely related to the third. He linked the work of the Spirit with ethical conduct and responsible living in community. The inner work of the Holy Spirit necessarily produces deeds of love and mercy.

When Wesley and his followers were charged with neglecting Christian duties, he replied that he had insisted continually "on all outward as well as all inward holiness." He appealed to the "whole tenor of our sermons, . . . in particular to those upon *Our Lord's Sermon on the Mount,* wherein every branch of gospel obedience is both asserted and proved to be indispensably necessary to eternal salvation."[7]

● Wesley's concern for personal religion was matched by *his passion for social religion.* As the historian John Wesley Bready has shown, this vital emphasis upon the activating power of the Holy Spirit became a mighty moral force in England and throughout the world. It transformed the antislavery leader Wilberforce. It inspired the so-called Clapham Sect of laymen who were committed to applying the ethic of Jesus to personal, political, national, and international affairs. It quickened innumerable persons, great

---

[7] *Letters,* IV, 330-31.

and small, to share in the work of bringing a new moral quality into large segments of society.

The Methodist emphasis on the vitalizing work of the Holy Spirit has been one of the most extensive efforts in the history of Christianity to moralize and spiritualize the nature of persons and their community affairs.

● Wesley never made the mistake of viewing the impulse toward responsible living in community as merely an expression of man's own higher aspirations. Rather, this passion was born of the Spirit. Wesley knew that the inner souls of people must be transformed and empowered from on high, that is, from God. He never wavered from this. Without it people were sure to sink like stones to the lowest levels of pride, greed, dishonesty, lust, mediocrity, and selfishness.

Thus, the life-transforming, community-changing power of the Spirit is to be understood in the context of the biblical revelation as a whole where the supernatural initiative of God is paramount. According to Wesley, this was not a matter of the struggling stream of duty nor of the fitful torrent of human aspiration but of the vast ocean of the divine release of energy through the Holy Spirit.

Not by accident did thirteen (one fourth) of Wesley's "standard sermons" deal with our Lord's Sermon on the Mount, for there Jesus' ethical teachings came to clear focus. When the primary concern is with actual righteousness—as it was with Wesley—persons inevitably turn to the Sermon on the Mount as an unrivaled source of practical guidance. Here again we have to be reminded that *Wesley never supposed that the divine requirements of the Sermon on the Mount could be realized apart from the Holy Spirit.* Nor did he imagine that the Kingdom could be realized in any final sense in this present world.

This general emphasis on both personal righteousness and community responsibility is one of the distinctive contributions of the Wesleyan heritage to the Christian movement. More will be said on this in Chapter 12.

THE HOLY SPIRIT AND PERSONAL SALVATION

6

The Holy Spirit and The Human Spirit

In this symbol the Holy Spirit descends on the cross
that rises from the sacramental vessel, while doves
symbolizing souls perch on the scrolls flanking the
cross.

We have seen that the Holy Spirit is God in his nearness
working to magnify Christ in us. This implies the comfort-
ing and challenging thought that a basic kinship exists
between God and us. Without this, how could there be
any experience of the divine presence or any empowerment
by the divine grace? The thought that we are kin to God
is one of the greatest teachings of the Bible.

Think of the difference in feeling between two people
who wake up in the morning: One feels estranged from
God, for he seems so far away. The other senses the nearness of God, for he seems so near, so closely related.

Two Mistaken Views

We find two major errors in ideas concerning the way
God and persons are related to each other.

The first is that they are so close to each other that our

souls are simply merged into the divine Being. According to this view, we are like drops of water in the ocean. We have no real identity. On this basis, then, our experience of selfhood is an illusion—for we are not individuals, we are tiny segments of God. According to this error, the human soul is totally merged into the divine Being. This is the extreme mystical view expressed in certain oriental religions and in various philosophies.

This idea is contrary to the Bible and to common sense. The Bible clearly emphasizes the identity of each individual. Abraham, though having faith in God, remained himself. So it was with Moses. And so also with Hannah. Even the prophets, such as Isaiah and Ezekiel, who had great visions of God, did not lose their own selfhood and identity. The Bible teaches that each person maintains a sacred line of selfhood.

Each soul is itself before God. God's plan does not provide for any soul to be merged into the divine Being like a drop of water in the ocean. This does not mean, however, that we cannot be one with God in purpose or in spirit.

What the Bible teaches, common sense confirms. We know by direct experience that we are ourselves. I am not you. You are not I. All conversation and daily relationships with other people assume that each person is himself. Each has his or her physical features. This is the way we recognize one another. Each has his or her own name. Your signature is your own. Large and small transactions regarding money and property are validated by signatures. These imply the unique individuality of each person.

Just as no person can be merged into another human being, so no one can be merged into God. The Bible and common sense will not allow us to lapse into this mystical error. Our relationship to the Holy Spirit, then, is person-to-person, not absorption or exclusion.

The biblical perspective on this has been beautifully expressed by a Mississippi poet, Perry Tanksley, in these words:

"For years each day at six A.M.
He went to church and bowed his knee
And meekly prayed, 'Dear God, it's Jim.'
And when he'd leave we all could see

The Presence came and walked with him.
As Jim grew old the chastening rod
Of years left him so ill and drawn
His path to church is now untrod;
But in his room each day at dawn
He hears a voice, 'Dear Jim, it's God!' "[1]

● A second error is just the opposite of the mystical idea. According to it, God is totally different from us. He is wholly other. No kinship whatever exists between him and us. According to this error, God is said to *transcend* (exist above and independent of) us in every way.

This too is contrary both to the Bible and to common sense. To be sure, as Creator, God is over and beyond us. God only is God, and we are creatures. But the Bible teaches that God is also present in his world and *with* his people. We are the sheep of his pasture. God acts in us, with us, and through us. If it were true that God was totally separated from us or totally different, we could not respond to him nor could we receive him into our hearts. Water and oil do not mix.

A Living Relationship

● We have seen that one of the most important works of the Holy Spirit is to *teach* us. He is the Spirit of truth. How could he enlighten our minds unless we could communicate with and understand each other? This implies kinship. We do not try to teach science or poetry to a dog. Why? No kinship exists between us at those points. We have seen also that the Holy Spirit convicts us of sin and wrongdoing. But how could this be possible if we were on a totally different wave length? A tree, a planet, a star, and a snake cannot be convicted of sin. Why not? They have no moral capacity. They do not bear any kinship to the convicting power of the Spirit.

The Holy Spirit guides and supports us in moral righteousness. This too implies that God made us the kind of beings who can participate in goodness. The great thinker Immanuel Kant said that persons have dignity because they are bearers of the moral law. This means that by God's

---

[1] "The Visitor," from *Love Gift*, by Perry Tanksley (Fleming H. Revell Company, 1971). Used by permission.

creation people have an inborn capacity for morality. Unless this were the case, one could never recognize the moral difference between Judas Iscariot and Jesus of Nazareth. How could the Holy Spirit convict one of sin if a person could not tell the difference btween love and hate, goodness and badness? How could Jesus Christ be revealed unless a human being could recognize the unutterable moral beauty of his life? Similarly, the Holy Spirit fills us with love for others. How would this be possible unless the divine love found an answering capacity in the human soul?

The teaching of the Bible, then, is that, without losing our identity, we have a mysterious kinship with the Holy Spirit that makes interaction possible.

● One further comment is needed to round out our understanding concerning our kinship with the Holy Spirit. This has to do with the basic fact that we are made for God.

The human soul requires God for its meaning and fulfillment. The biblical writers were not interested primarily in a correct understanding of the Holy Spirit; their main concern was with our *response* to God. They assumed that we were made for God and could never realize the purpose for which we were created without the new life and power of the Holy Spirit.

Our human nature, when unaided by the Holy Spirit, is unable to enter upon its God-appointed pilgrimage. We are inevitably unhappy and misplaced in the world until we open our lives to the presence and power of the Holy Spirit.

In what I consider the profoundest comment on our human nature ever uttered outside the Bible, Augustine said: "Thou hast made us for Thyself, O God, and our hearts are restless till they rest in Thee."

Many people may require years of negative experiences to see this. Some see it only in fleeting glimpses. Tolstoi, at a time when he had attained fame and fortune, struggled for two long years before he came to see that "God is that one without whom we cannot live." During this period of struggle someone said of him that he was going and not arriving, seeking and not finding—a God-haunted man. Therefore, it is not enough merely to say that each human being is made for God. We need to ask what this profound fact signifies about our strange lives on this obscure little planet. Also, what does it mean regarding our relationship with God?

One meaning, as Wesley saw, is that the Holy Spirit is present in everyone of us from the start. This yearning *is not something we have produced but what God has put into our hearts.* Thus, the Holy Spirit is present in our yearning for the Infinite.

Often this need for God is obscured by our selfishness and our distractions. But underneath all of these and other factors lies this mysterious yearning for God.

● The Holy Spirit is active as a primary initiating presence in every phase of the soul's spiritual pilgrimage. He prepares the way for the new birth. He moves and stirs within the soul to aid in the never ceasing quest for the fullest experiences of divine grace. He bears witness along the way to his presence within. And always he ties together his inner presence with the outer deeds.

The Holy Spirit and The New Birth

Many people tend to assume that our deepest needs can be met by education, politeness, job skills, and social order. They recognize also that we need fellowship with one another, recreation for a change of pace, and touches of beauty to adorn life.

These people, however, seem to have a certain blindness to what Jesus had in mind when he said to Nicodemus, "Truly, truly, I say to you, unless one is born anew, he cannot see the kingdom of God." (John 3:3) Let us have no doubt as to the importance of education, refinement, skills, and the rest. These have their appropriate roles. The question is, Can they satisfy the deepest needs of people as God sees them and as we experience them?

The tendency to resist the biblical teaching on the new birth is particularly evident in people who have attained considerable success in the secular world. More than that, we seem to have a kind of natural resistance to it because we do not want to come to grips with the *moral* issues of life.

In contrast to our resistance to the whole idea of the new birth the Bible emphasizes the necessity of it. But do we really need it? Do people who are looking toward the twenty-first century need to concern themselves with the new birth? Is it not archaic, old-fashioned, out of date?

Our Need for New Birth

Everything depends on whether we recognize the limits of human efforts and are willing to let the Holy Spirit move in our lives. We are made for God and can never be satisfied without him. More specifically, the Bible teaches not only that we are made for God but that we are so made that we can never come to fulfillment apart from the *goodness* of God.

The biblical writers will never let us forget that morality and religion go together. God is good. He is altogether righteous. He is perfect love. He wants his children to come to grips with the *moral* issues of their existence as his creatures. According to Jesus, what God most wants is for the human soul to be motivated by God's love.

If we consider only what people want in relation to their earthly affairs, the new birth becomes an irrelevant intrusion. Christmas and Easter are reduced to special days on a secular calendar. The whole realm of the divine initiative would be ruled out as a grand delusion. But if we get a vision of what *God* wants of us, the new birth becomes the beginning of a truly new life with God. What Jesus said to Nicodemus comes home to us as well.

● According to the Bible, God wants the minds and souls of persons to embody and express his love. Jesus made this clear by example and precept. God has made known what he expects of us. We can have no question that this love does not rule naturally in our souls. How then does God's purpose for us begin? The biblical answer is, Through the new birth. Not by education nor by common civilities nor by any long, extended course of study or action are we motivated by God's love. Rather, it is by faith coupled with *a basic policy decision* to let God have his way with us, come what may. Before such a policy decision is made, we should experience heart-searching, repentance, forgiveness, and faith.

Here is where the Holy Spirit comes in. Since God wants us to come to grips with the moral realities of our existence, and since he made us to find our meaning and destiny only in and through his love, his Holy Spirit acts to assist us in realizing this. Thus the work of the Holy Spirit in preparing us for the new birth is no incidental matter; it is a primary concern of the Spirit.

The Spirit and the Meaning of Daily Experiences

How, specifically, does the Holy Spirit act to move us toward the new birth? In several ways.

● First, the Holy Spirit illuminates our minds so that, whether gradually or suddenly, we see *the religious or spiritual meaning of our varied experiences*. Everyone has certain recurring experiences that are loaded with meaning: boredom, loneliness, fear, misunderstanding, tragedy, bereavement, remorse, guilt, hope, joy, peace. But for the secularist who says, "If God is, he does not matter," the deeper meaning of these experiences is lost. For example, in the understanding of the secularist the experience of boredom is what it is and nothing more. But in the biblical context, *the Holy Spirit is trying to say something through the language of boredom.* The great question concerning all major ranges of experience is, *What do they signify by being experienced?* The Holy Spirit gives a deeper meaning that goes far beyond the bare experienced fact.

Negative Aspects of Life

● The whole network of our negative experiences becomes a kind of language that the Holy Spirit wants to use to draw us into the orbit of God's love.

Do we feel guilty when we are guilty? This is the Spirit's way of reminding us that we were made to come to terms with God's goodness and his moral order. Do we feel the distressing pain of fear or the uneasiness of a deep-seated anxiety? This is the Spirit's language calling us to the mysterious freedom from fear that comes through love and faith in God. Boredom? From the standpoint of revealed religion, this is an obvious summons to find meaning and joy by attaching ourselves to the ultimate Source of mean-

81

ing. Are we lonely? This is God's call to that communion of Spirit with spirit which fulfills.

None of this is to deny our need for human companionship. Nor is it to minimize the value of working relationships in this earthly setting. Everyone needs something to do, someone to love, and something earthly to live for. To love and be loved is basic. The point is, however, that over and beyond this, these negative experiences are the Spirit's call to the faith relationship to God. The Holy Spirit seeks to make us aware of this need by revealing the deeper meaning of our negative experiences.

● The Holy Spirit leads us to take another step toward the new birth which is closely related to this. The Spirit helps us *have a clear and undoubting awareness of the inability of any and all of the offerings of this temporal realm to satisfy our deepest needs*. Without this sense of the inadequacy of this world, who would call upon the Lord? With it, who would not?

We may turn to nature and, for all of its beauties and usefulness, it cannot satisfy the soul. Or we may drink from the fountains of culture and civilization and receive some gratification, but our deeper thirst remains unquenched. Or we may turn with the existentialists toward ourselves and say, "We will to live!" But, alas, we know that we are whistling in the dark. The Holy Spirit is present to remind us of the radical ineptness of this temporal sphere to satisfy.

> "Whither shall I go from thy Spirit?
> Or whither shall I flee from thy presence?
> If I ascend to heaven, thou art there!
> If I make my bed in Sheol, thou art there!"
> (Psalms 139:7-8)

Earlier in the twentieth century people dreamed of inevitable progress. Some persons supposed that science and technology would answer all our needs. But two world wars, the Vietnam experience, and numberless other violent outbursts have reminded us that science and technology cannot come to grips with the deeper issues of human life. The recurring scandals in politics, business, labor, family life, and in nearly every arena—not to mention the personal disasters from the breakdown of character—remind us of the deep-seated difficulties within human nature itself. Educated and cultured people are no less sinful than the ignorant and uncouth. Indeed, people often use their advantages in education, money, and culture to run interference for their pride, meanness, and self-indulgence. This is especially true where money, sex, power, and social status are concerned.

● Contemporary people have often lived under the illusion that they can get away with anything. For many of them no moral order exists. Hence, in regard to work, money, sex, recreation, and the like, anything goes. For example, they suppose that temporary romantic attachments can be as fulfilling, or more so, than the enduring commitments of an authentic marriage. But, as life goes on, they find that they forgot something—the law of consequences. Superficial attachments breed superficial experiences. Passing interests produce transient gratifications. On the other side, great loyalties make possible ever enriching experiences of meaning and joy. As Bishop Joseph Butler, of eighteenth-century England, said, "Things and actions are what they are, and the consequences of them will be what they will be; why then should we desire to be deceived?" We reap what we sow.

What is the meaning of these experiences? From them the Holy Spirit helps us understand the necessity for a radical transformation *within* the souls of people. And if we remain blind to this illuminating process of the Holy Spirit, we continue in darkness, and in that state we are indeed children of darkness rather than of light. "And this is the judgment, that the light has come into the world, and men loved darkness rather than light, because their deeds were evil." (John 3:19)

Positive Aspects of Life

On the positive side, the Holy Spirit works through conscience and the lure of the ideal. Human nature is a curious mixture of good and bad, love and hate, excitement and boredom. In this total process we have something like an instinctive capacity to respond to the ideal. Goodness, beauty, and truth are ideal values in all civilizations. Our human longing to weave these into our lives is matched by a yearning for all the help we can get in the process, for we find ourselves at war with ourselves here.

Paul knew this when he said, "I do not understand my own actions. For I do not do what I want, but I do the very thing I hate. . . . I can will what is right, but I cannot do it." (Romans 7:15, 18) Still, there is always this pull of the best in us.

If we do not care deeply about this lure of the ideal and our failure to follow it, the matter is settled. We remain children of darkness, shut off from the Spirit. *We do not require the grace of God to be mediocre persons.*

If we care, as Paul did, then we begin to open ourselves to the new alternative—the magnificent possibility—that our heavenly Father wants to assist us in the adventures toward the ideal. The Holy Spirit assists us to be open at last to the grace of God. The beginning of all this movement toward the grace of God is the new birth.

The Spirit and Repentance

The Holy Spirit helps us repent. This is a central focus of the Spirit's activity. As long as we are complacent, arrogant, and unbending in our selfish ways, we cannot pass from the darkness into the light. Why should we repent? Not primarily because we have broken specific commandments. Rather, because we have allowed ourselves to turn away from God and his purpose for us. We have forgotten the "dear Father" relationship that Jesus had with God. We have fallen far short of the glory of God in Christ. We are to repent because we are out of line with God.

Repentance takes us back to the bedrock of essential honesty with ourselves and God. We quit passing the buck. We stop deceiving ourselves by supposing that it does not matter how we live. No one can go deeper than honest confession of sin to God. Here we strike the solid rock on which God can rebuild the soul. Then the Holy Spirit moves into our hearts to enable us to repent. At the same time, our own wills may be at work bearing us in the same direction.

• We cannot truly repent unless we have absolute confidence in God's graciousness to accept and forgive. Again, the Holy Spirit meets our spirits and enables us to have the faith whereby God graciously forgives.

The Spirit and Our Policy Decision

In and through our experiences and Spirit-relationships emerges *that profound policy decision to open our lives to the leadership of Jesus Christ our Savior.* Whenever we truly behold the glory of God and his self-giving love in Jesus Christ, we want to make that policy decision. Indeed, we feel strongly moved to do so. The Holy Spirit mysteriously interacts with our own free wills to help us make this life-shaking response to God. Then, and only then, God's forgiving grace flows into our souls in life-transforming power. We are new creations by the power of the Spirit. We have moved into a new dimension of existence. We are born anew by divine grace. As Paul said, "Therefore, if any one is in Christ, he is a new creation; the old has passed away, behold, the new has come." (2 Corinthians 5:17)

This new birth is the beginning of the great spiritual pilgrimage toward the never ending quest for expressions of perfect love which, according to the Bible, is God's sublime goal for all his children. Of that sanctifying work of the Holy Spirit we shall have more to say after pausing to consider the witness of the Spirit.

The Witness
Of the Spirit

The fish was used as a secret symbol by Christians
in times of persecution. The initial letters of the
Greek words for "Jesus Christ, Son of God, Savior"
spell "fish."

Jesus promised his disciples that he would send the
Spirit. His life, teaching, passion, death, and resurrection
bore a magnificent witness to the gracious availability of
God to all who believe and open their souls to him. Under-
lying the New Testament teaching on the witness of the
Spirit is the foundation of confidence and assurance which
Jesus laid. He is the final guarantor of that experienced
sense of God's presence and power in the souls of men.

New Testament Affirmations

Against this background, the apostles and others in the
New Testament affirmed clearly and without hesitation the

presence of the Holy Spirit in their lives. They *knew* that the promised Spirit was at work in them because they felt his presence and manifested his power in their deeds.

● Paul was the master spokesman on this theme when he said, "For all who are led by the Spirit of God are sons of God. For you did not receive the spirit of slavery to fall back into fear, but you have received the spirit of sonship. When we cry, 'Abba! Father!' it is the Spirit himself bearing witness with our spirit that we are children of God, and if children, then heirs, heirs of God and fellow heirs with Christ, provided we suffer with him in order that we may also be glorified with him." (Romans 8:15-17)

Here are three thoughts of first importance:

First, Paul uses the present tense. All who are led by the Spirit are—now—the children of God. The Spirit bears witness with our spirit that we *are* the children of God. This means that the witness of Spirit to our being in the family of God is *a presently experienced reality*.

The second thought is that this experience of God's presence has been given to us and *received*. "You have received the spirit of sonship." (Romans 8:15) The witness of the Spirit is not a human concoction but a divine gift. We, of course, must receive it.

The third thought is that this witness of the Spirit is directly connected with our conduct and our destiny in the future. Paul says that we are heirs of God and fellow heirs with Christ, *provided* we suffer with him. This means that we are led by the self-giving spirit of the cross. The children of God are to inherit the Kingdom prepared for them, if they are faithful. Thus the witness of the Spirit has to do with *our present salvation and does not guarantee that we will persevere* unto a greater destiny in the kingdom of heaven, for all are in danger of backsliding and thus losing the experience of salvation and the witness to it.

● In addition to the general reports concerning the experiences of Peter and the others, certain passages in First John support Paul's testimony.

"See what love the Father has given us, that we should be called children of God; and so we are. . . . Beloved, we are God's children now; it does not yet appear what we shall be, but we know that when he appears we shall be like him, for we shall see him as he is." (1 John 3:1*a*, 2)

"So we know and believe the love God has for us. God is love, and he who abides in love abides in God, and God abides in him. In this is love perfected with us, that we may have confidence for the day of judgment, because as he is so are we in this world. . . . We love, because he first loved us. If any one says, 'I love God,' and hates his brother, he is a liar; for he who does not love his brother whom he has seen, cannot love God whom he has not seen." (1 John 4:16-17, 19-20)

These passages are witness not merely to a doctrine believed but to a reality experienced. They assume that God's love in us is a gift to be received. Here also is the ethical context of a Christlike love that binds us to good deeds here and a great destiny in the life after death.

This witness of the Spirit carries with it the magnificent God-given assurance of the ultimate triumph of righteousness. Those who have faith are given this assurance provided they participate with God in doing the work of love.

Christians of Other Eras

These composite realities of experience, which we speak of under the term "the witness of the Spirit," have been attested to by Christians of all generations. The devotional literature of every era bears repeated witness to what Paul and others said in the earliest days.

Augustine in his *Confessions* gave utterance to this theme. Even Luther, when he was at his best, expressed the sense of assurance with great joy. Yet his followers did not put any special emphasis on it. Calvin, quite understandably, recognized this inner witness of the Spirit as a possibility but gave little attention to it because he believed that God had already chosen the elect. This sense of being among the elect was a mere trifle compared to God's decision. And it became a problem to know whether or not one was really among the elect. Thus the term "witness of the Spirit" in Reformation theology referred not so much to the inner assurance of personal salvation as to testimony to the authority of the Bible. That theme is important but is beside the point here.

● As was the case with very few others, John Wesley picked up this theme concerning the inner witness and gave it an important place in his preaching and teaching. The primary reason for this was that it was based on both Scripture and experience. The Christian life, he said, cannot be based on a speculative principle, such as election, because nobody could *know* on that basis whether or not he was among the redeemed. Only God would know.

I would not go as far as to say that the idea of the inner witness was the fundamental contribution of Methodism to the life and thought of the church. But it was important in Wesley's thought and experience.

Wesley defined "the witness of the Spirit" in his famous sermon on that topic as follows: ". . . the testimony of the Spirit is an inward impression on the soul, whereby the Spirit of God directly witnesses to my spirit, that I am a child of God; that Jesus Christ hath loved me, and given Himself for me; and that all my sins are blotted out, and I, even I, am reconciled to God." [1] He goes on to liken it to that kind of practical certainty that all persons experience when they actually see and feel something.

Confirming Paul's great statement, Wesley says, "The Spirit of God does give a believer such a testimony of his adoption, that while it is present to the soul, he can no more doubt the reality of his sonship, than he can doubt of the shining of the sun, while he stands in the full blaze of his beams." [2] This witness of the Spirit then becomes a source not only of the Christian's joy but also of love for God and people.

This teaching, which had become obscured in Roman Catholicism, neglected in the Church of England, and bypassed by the Reformers, was recovered by Wesley on the basis of Scripture and his own experience.

Perhaps Wesley was also influenced by his father's personal testimony during his last illness. At that time his father said, "The inward witness, son, the inward witness, . . . that is proof, the strongest proof of Christianity." [3]

● As Wesley knew, everyone needs to be aware of certain dangers in this matter. The biblical writers themselves warned against them, for it is easy to claim the witness of the Spirit without showing the fruits of it. We read,

---

[1] *The Standard Sermons of John Wesley*, I, 208.
[2] *Standard Sermons*, II, 210.
[3] *Letters*, II, 135.

"Beloved, do not believe every spirit, but test the spirits to see whether they are of God; for many false prophets have gone out into the world. By this you know the Spirit of God: every spirit which confesses that Jesus Christ has come in the flesh is of God, and every spirit which does not confess Jesus is not of God." (1 John 4:1-3a) Paul said, "But let each one test his own work . . ." (Galatians 6:4) The law of sowing and reaping was basic with him. (6:7)

Wesley recognized another danger. Some people had said that this inner witness meant the assurance that a person would persevere to the end. In response to a minister by the name of Bedford, Wesley wrote: "We speak of an assurance of our present pardon; not, as he does, of our final perseverance." [4] *We are given no assurance of once in grace always in grace.* We are assured of salvation *presently* experienced.

● An early Evangelical United Brethren theologian, S. J. Gamertsfelder, affirms, as Wesley did, the function of the Holy Spirit in providing an inner personal witness when writing about justification and regeneration. He writes: "The Holy Spirit makes the Christian life a matter of conscious experience in the heart of the believer. He sustains, educates, and perfects the Divine life in every soul that responds to the Divine call." [5]

Gamertsfelder does insist, however, that while the Holy Spirit "follows man and calls repeatedly to elicit a response from the human heart . . . the Christian life does not begin in reality until there is some form of interaction [response] on the part of man." [6]

All Christians need to recognize a further danger, as did Wesley and other early leaders—such as Gamertsfelder, who reflected the insights of Jacob Albright and Philip Otterbein—in the various streams of denominational life which preceded our present United Methodist Church. This danger involved a merely personal experience of assurance disconnected from the reality of God's action in Christ and from man's responsible living. Wesley protected his teaching by placing it within the total setting of the biblical

---

[4] *The Journal of John Wesley,* II, 82-83.
[5] *Systematic Theology,* by S. J. Gamertsfelder (Abingdon Press, reprint 1938), p. 474. Out of print.
[6] *Ibid.*

revelation. He did so also by insisting that this inner witness must be supported by a clear conscience before God and by doing deeds that necessarily flow from God's love. To avoid running into endless error and delusion, Wesley said simply that the genuineness of the witness of the Spirit is seen in its fruits.

Is Inner Witness Necessary?

Two intimately interrelated questions need to be looked at: Is this inner witness necessary for personal salvation? Is every Christian expected to experience the witness of the Spirit all the time?

● In response to the first question, the answer is No. The New Testament does not teach that the witness of the Spirit is a principle of salvation. We are not brought into the life-giving relationship with God through Christ by this inner witness—this happens only through repentance and faith. Anyone who actually trusts in God's forgiving love and empowering grace in Jesus Christ *is* redeemed regardless of what he may feel. But, as Paul and others said, this inner witness is a normal and appropriate experience when we have faith. The inner joy and witness to our salvation tends to go with the awareness of what God has done for us and in us. Besides this, the *fact* of God's presence and power is normally an experienced reality.

In his earlier days Wesley taught that every Christian necessarily felt this inner assurance as an accompanying factor in the Christian life. Later he modified this. He was wise. We are dealing with the strange elements of our varied experiences and moods as human beings. We ought not overlook the plain fact of experience that this sense of God's presence may come and go, depending upon our varied moods and circumstances.

● This much is sure: God wants his children to *know* of his boundless love in Christ and, from time to time, he gives them the blessed assurance of his love and care. Sometimes this comes in our solitary moments of devotion, sometimes as we worship in the community of faith, sometimes when we are walking through the shadowlands of bereavement, sometimes while we are struggling in the thick of life to conquer temptation or to serve our fellow beings. But God forever holds out the promise of this recurring witness of the Spirit to all who fulfill the conditions of the spiritual life.

The witness of the Spirit remains with us, for the most part, in proportion to *our faithfulness and growth as Christians*. When we fail to grow in grace and our faith falters from neglect, the inner witness departs. The Holy Spirit always wants us to grow and adventure in the purposes of God. The riches of divine grace are limitless. God wants us to abound more and more in his love and in creative service to his children.

The witness of the Spirit comes again and again to those who, like Paul, "press on toward the goal for the prize of the upward call of God in Christ Jesus." (Philippians 3:14)

9

The Creative Power Of the Spirit

The seven doves surrounding the cross represent the seven gifts of the Spirit: power, wealth, wisdom, might, honor, glory, and blessing. (Revelation 5:12)

The terms *sanctification* and *Christian perfection* have been used to identify the highest levels of Christian experience (inner holiness). They express a profound truth based upon realities affirmed in Scripture and confirmed in experience. The language may not be the best for these times, but the reality of God's call to perfection needs to be heard by people of all generations.

This divine summons to perfection must be seen in the context of the total biblical vision of God's purpose for his children. Otherwise, it will be reduced to a sect-type emphasis, one-sided, peculiar, impractical. The revealed purpose of God for all men is that they be redeemed from their sins by grace and that they be re-created by grace so they may express the love of God in Christ. That is, God wants all people to be saved and to manifest that fact through deeds of love and mercy. (Ephesians 2)

The Meaning of Being Saved

To be saved, of course, means *to be right with God.* It means being forgiven by grace through faith and committed to moving with God. This implies inner rightness with ourselves—inner integrity, quality of character, the love of Christ within. At the same time it means rightness with our fellow human beings.

If we leave the matter there, we are apt to miss the dynamic dimensions of the Spirit in the total process of personal salvation. The Bible teaches that God is through and through dynamic, active, creative, headed somewhere. The Bible has no room for the notion of a static deity. To be sure, God is from everlasting to everlasting the same. He is always himself. He is good. He is love. "His steadfast love endures for ever." (Psalms 100:5) His character never changes. His purpose for his children and his faithfulness endure to all generations. In and through all of this—and indeed because of it—God is dynamic and creative.

Against this background, what does it really mean to be saved? Two things at least.

First, it means a life-giving personal faith in God as our Father as made known in Jesus Christ. This implies communion with God. It means the sense of joy in his presence. It means friendship with God. And, as we have seen, it means inner integrity and quality of soul. Along with this, there is the sense of awe, mystery, and wonder in the presence of God. To be saved also implies the assurance of firm conviction that death cannot break the ties that bind us thus to God, for God has established them. To be saved in this sense, then, is an end in itself.

Personal salvation has a second meaning. We have seen that to be saved is to be right with God and people. But if God is concerned about his children, how can we fail to join him in that concern? *If God wants certain goals achieved for his children, can we be right with him and ignore his aims?* Of course not. Jesus showed the way here.

He rejoiced in the fellowship with the Father. He also carried out the Father's purpose to redeem the world.

God wants us to enjoy him forever. He wants us also to do his will. No soul is truly saved who does not both enjoy friendship with God and strive to carry out his aims.

We Are Made for Growth

● At every stage we are creatures before whom there are countless *unrealized possibilities*. The God who made us, and whose we are, does not ignore this. He summons the redeemed always to realize those possibilities opened up through Christ. He wants us to realize and to express these as long as we live. Can we be right with God and ignore the possibilities for growth he sets before us? Of course not.

If God is working toward goals, he wants us to work toward these goals with him. To be saved, or to be right with God, then, means to be *moving* with God, to be seeking his goals, carrying out his aims, realizing and helping others realize the new possibilities in Christ. His aims are always based on his character. God has revealed his goodness and love in Jesus Christ. Therefore, the primary possibilities that God envisions for us have to do with the never-ceasing growth in love.

To be right with God means to yearn for more love, for increasing skill in expressing that love, and for the growth in wisdom essential to the work of love. The Christian can in no way neglect the moral demands of life and remain true to Jesus Christ.

● Before we turn to the mission of the Holy Spirit in the higher levels of the Christian life, we need to observe a very important fact about the human soul. I have in mind the fact that it is *open-ended* regarding the future. The past is closed. The future, open. The soul is not a fixed entity. A stone is a stone. It is a fixed entity. It cannot grow. A tree is a tree. It can develop only so far and no farther. A dog is a dog. This is true even though there may be new tricks and some limited new possibilities. Dogs, birds, and even insects can do things that we cannot, but their capacities in the moral and spiritual realm are nothing compared to those of people.

We must never lose sight of our creatureliness. We are

ever dependent on God. Nevertheless, a human being has *limitless possibilities for growth and creative advance in moral and spiritual values.* God made us that way. Therefore, any normal human being can learn a new verse or read a new book or find a new way of dealing with an old problem or help people in new efforts or go deeper in understanding Jesus Christ, and so on. We stand before an open door of many possibilities for good. We must never forget that God is not only the Creator and Sustainer of the universe and people. He is also the Ground of all possibilities for good.

God in his infinite love and wisdom created us for growth. He has made known to us that our pilgrimage through this world requires constant growth and creative advance. He is made unhappy when we stop growing, for he did not create us to die on the vine. Can we be right with God and fail to hear his call to creative advances in goodness and love? Of course not. "We are God's children now; it does not yet appear what we shall be." (1 John 3:2)

What can be more important than the presence of the Holy Spirit to assist us in these creative advances in Christian experience and service? We may not be assuming too much to say that *for this purpose* all the biblical revelation, all the work of Christ, and all the resources of the Spirit have been brought to our attention.

The Spirit's Supreme Goal for Us

For Luther and others the heart of the Christian religion was justification by faith. Everything revolved around that. Perhaps we should take another look at this doctrine. This is not to suggest that we should modify or minimize the profound biblical teaching that we are forgiven by grace through faith and not by our works. The decisive point here is that our works *do not function* as the principle of salvation. They have no *merit* in relation to God's forgiveness. They do not bring us into the right relationship with God. This we steadfastly believe.

● Is justification by faith (forgiveness through faith) the heart of the Christian religion? It is indispensable. It is the doorway into the kingdom of God. It leads to the new birth. But is the birth of a baby the final fact about that infant? Without the birth nothing else could happen. But the mere fact of the birth, without growth and development, is of little consequence. So it is with God's forgiving grace and the new birth. These are the promises of greater things yet to come.

In a sense "justification by faith" is a more realistic term than "new birth," for we need to be forgiven again and again in the ongoing of life. Always we are forgiven by

God's grace in Jesus Christ through faith. Yet the term "new birth" rightly refers to that fundamental experience of being re-created by the Spirit through Jesus Christ. This, along with the forgiveness of our sins, is that grand beginning from which we move with the Spirit toward the ever deepening and expanding adventures with God.

At this point I am inclined to agree with H. Wheeler Robinson when he says that the doctrine of justification by faith was not the central focus of Paul's teaching:

"The increasing recognition that the doctrine of the Holy Spirit is central in the Christian thought of the Apostle Paul (rather than the Rabbinical doctrine of 'justification') marks a great advance in the interpretation of his Gospel. Every other conception of his is baptized into this, and most of all the concrete fact of history—the Cross of Christ. The whole life of the Christian, normal and abnormal, is brought within the sphere of the Holy Spirit." [1]

[1] Fom *The Christian Experience of the Holy Spirit*, by H. Wheeler Robinson (James Nisbet & Co. Ltd, 1928), p. 62.

When we understand John Wesley's thought more deeply, we begin to see that he was moving within the larger sphere of the universal, or catholic, tradition in his emphasis on the sanctifying power of the Holy Spirit. He joined Paul in emphasizing the power of the Spirit to re-create persons for righteous living. This encompasses and moves beyond the heritage of the Reformation.

● Quite possibly the most important contribution of the heritage of Methodism to the Christian world is the way in which this emphasis on sanctity, or scriptural holiness, or Christian perfection—whatever the term used—has been unfolded.

Wesley himself, even before his conversion, felt compelled to dedicate himself wholly to God. No halfway measure would do. But he carried out his program at first by relying primarily on his own resources. After his conversion, which must never be minimized, his early interest in holiness of life was *taken out of the realm of duty and placed in the sphere of grace*. Holiness, or Christian perfection, was not a human achievement but an *ever increasing presence of the Holy Spirit*.

That this was the plain teaching of Scripture he never doubted throughout his ministry. When Wesley's teaching on Christian perfection is understood for what it is, it will be seen not as some strange doctrine to be left to the various sects. Rather, it will be viewed as an authentic account of what God has revealed in Christ to be his primary aim for his children.

Wesley's Understanding of "Perfection"

In his work entitled "A Plain Account of Christian Perfection," Wesley tells what he did and did not mean. Certainly, he did not mean a fixed state of the soul. He knew as well as anyone that the soul is made to grow in grace and to adventure into the future with God. In this use, "perfection" does not mean a finished product. Christian growth begins on earth and continues "to all eternity." He knew also that people are bound to make mistakes of judgment. One and all, they live out their lives within vast ranges of ignorance. Moreover, he knew that as long as persons have freedom of will they can backslide. He was aware that human beings always stand in need of God's forgiveness and of the means of grace which the Holy Spirit provides through public worship, preaching, the sacraments, prayer, the study of the Bible, and service to others.

● Wesley was fully aware of the dangers standing in the way of all who take seriously God's call toward perfection, or holiness. So he said, "Beware of that daughter of pride, enthusiasm [fanaticism]. O keep at the utmost distance from it! Give no place to a heated imagination. Do not hastily ascribe things to God. Do not easily suppose dreams, voices, impressions, visions, or revelations to be from God." [2]

What Wesley had in mind was nothing more or less than what Jesus taught, namely, "the loving God with all our heart and soul, and our neighbor as ourselves. It is love governing the heart and life, running through all tempers, words, and actions." [3] Love becomes "the sole principle of action." [4] This implies the constant readiness to do good wherever and whenever possible. According to Wesley, one of the principal rules of religion is to serve God on every occasion.

● How is this experience possible? It is possible only through the presence and power of the Holy Spirit who works in us and through us to realize the divine purpose for our lives. That purpose is not merely to encourage people to seek values on their own. Rather, it is to realize moral and spiritual values through the mysterious interaction of the divine and the human.

We hear a lot of talk these days about being fully human. This is a helpful way of suggesting that the supreme moral aim in life is self-realization. Since we cannot realize our highest selves apart from others, to be fully human involves compassionate concern for others. While good, this misses the deeper dimensions of revealed or biblical religion.

The greatest practical teaching of the Bible is this: God made us for himself, and he is always available to help us in the moral and spiritual pilgrimage toward the kingdom of heaven. His aim for us includes two things, namely, *being* and *doing*.

---

[2] *Works*, XI, 429.
[3] *Works*, XI, 397.
[4] *Works*, XI, 395.

THE HOLY SPIRIT AND CHRISTIAN EXPERIENCE

"Being" and "Doing"

● *Being* has to do with the quality of soul. Goethe once said, "One must *be* something to *do* something." A bad character produces bad deeds. The inner quality of a human being is basic, This is why the New Testament writers speak of the new birth, the new creation, and the like. When we stress this inner quality of soul—inner rightness, integrity, purity of motive—the terms *sanctification, holiness,* and *Christian perfection* are especially appropriate, for they focus on this inner purity of soul in which God himself is interested.

In this context the concern is always with sanctification, for God is holy, pure, perfect. And the words of Jesus have their ageless relevance: "You, therefore, must be perfect, as your heavenly Father is perfect." (Matthew 5:48) The *aim* of the Christian must always be in the direction of God's perfect love and concern. Toward what other moral aim can we point? For this reason, through two thousand years of history Christians have been reminded to cultivate the life of prayer and meditation. Only as we return to Christ and what he represents does the Holy Spirit purify and move us toward rightness of purpose or Christian love.

The biblical teaching is not that we can purify ourselves but that the Holy Spirit moves mysteriously in the human soul to refine and purify it through Jesus Christ. To be fully and genuinely human, then, is always to be open to the inflowing grace of God. No one can be truly himself without God, for God has made us to adore him and to seek the perfection that only he can fully enjoy. But we can participate with him in that perfect love by the mysterious re-creative powers of the Holy Spirit. We can do this, however, only as long as the Holy Spirit continues to assist us. We may backslide. We may return to the universal practice of "going it alone"—without God. But as long as we are receptive to the Spirit, we continue to be new creations in Christ.

● Now, what about *doing?* When we move into the sphere of action, we leave such terms as *sanctification, holiness,* and *Christian perfection.* The soul may be sanctified or holy or characterized by perfect love in intention, but these terms properly apply to *being* rather than *acting.*

The genuine Christian is necessarily concerned with

deeds, for they are an expression of the inner quality of soul or character. The Holy Spirit works in us that we may do all the good we can. Since God aims toward the improvement of life, as Jesus showed, we are summoned to carry out those aims.

Granting the rightness of the motive and of the goal, we have only two real questions about a deed: (1) Does it accomplish the goal? (2) Is it the best way of doing so? These are questions of fact and of good or bad judgment. We need to pray daily for wisdom and good sense as well as for inner purity of purpose.

THE HOLY SPIRIT AND
THE CHRISTIAN LIFE

10

The Holy Spirit and Christian Habits

We have seen that the Holy Spirit is always available to assist us in the moral and spiritual life. Indeed, he is eager to help in all concerns having to do with our strength of body, mind, and soul. The Holy Spirit, being God, is perfect love. He is present to aid us in our daily work and in all important aspects of life. Supremely, he is with us in the quest for righteousness and the service to our fellow human beings which flows from it. This is a part of God's good news in Jesus Christ.

Certain *conditions* must be met if we are to receive this divine help. The Holy Spirit does not force his way into our lives. Even in the forgiveness of our sins, wherein we are justified before God, certain conditions must be fulfilled. We must be honest enough to repent. We must do our part in trusting God, through Christ, to forgive us. To be sure, as we have seen, the Holy Spirit helps us have this justifying faith. But we too have our part to play. In every step of the Christian life certain requirements must be met. Just as we have laws of nature, so we have laws of the spiritual life.

Means of Grace

We need to remember that John Wesley broke away from the Moravians early in his career in England because they minimized the means of grace—certain acts and relationships conducive to receiving the help of the Spirit. They stressed the free movement of the Spirit and underplayed public worship, the sacraments, Bible study, preaching and teaching, and deeds of service to humankind. Consequently, after preaching a series of sermons on these topics, Wesley took those who agreed with him and formed his own kind of society. *Everyone,* he insisted, *needs regularized means of grace to continue under the influence of the Spirit.*

● Both Scripture and common sense indicate the practical necessity of the means of grace. Otherwise, the spiritual life is left to the mercy of whim and chance. God is not the Lord of the whimsical and arbitrary.

I love the mountains. I like to see them early in the day when the morning sun kisses their brows. I like to see them also in the evening when, like sleeping giants, they lie tucked away under the cover of darkness. But I look out of my study window in Jackson, Mississippi, and I do not see the mountains. Why not? It is not that the mountains do not exist. It is that I have not put myself in a position to see them. So it is with us and God.

Jesus said, "Ask, and it will be given you; seek, and you will find; knock, and it will be opened to you." (Matthew 7:7) The conditions are that we must ask, seek, knock. This means that we must *desire earnestly* what God has for us. It means also that we must seek the Spirit's help in ways that have been made known to us through Jesus Christ and the Christian heritage.

Here is where the means of grace come in. Some people imagine that the Holy Spirit will just come upon them and dwell in them without the habits of Christian living. They are fundamentally mistaken. The Spirit's actions cannot be boxed in or restricted to any one formula. As Jesus said,

"The wind blows where it wills, and you hear the sound of it, but you do not know whence it comes or whither it goes; so it is with every one who is born of the Spirit." (John 3:8) This does not imply, however, that the Spirit acts whimsically. He always expresses himself as love and in love. His work is mysterious, not arbitrary. Jesus said to Nicodemus that he had to be born again of the Spirit. And he called upon him to fulfill the *conditions* necessary for being born of the Spirit.

Jesus' Teaching

Jesus taught his followers to prepare the soul to receive God's promised help. He went to the synagogue on the Sabbath day, as was his custom. He returned again and again to the Temple in Jerusalem. He thus used the available means of grace. He prayed regularly. This is a means of grace. He read the Scriptures and reflected on them. This is a means of grace. He lost no opportunity for doing good. Service to others is also a means of grace. God helps those who put themselves in a position to receive his grace.

The Christian life has to be built up. It does not just happen. It involves a continuing openness to the Spirit and a never ceasing yearning to be strengthened and empowered by the Spirit. This means paying attention to the daily call of God. It means prayer, Bible study, meditation, giving of time and means. It means growth.

To change the figure of speech, building a Christian life involves building on a solid foundation. As Jesus said, "Every one then who hears these words of mine and does them will be like a wise man who built his house upon the rock; and the rain fell, and the floods came, and the winds blew and beat upon that house, but it did not fall, because it had been founded on the rock." (Matthew 7:24-25)

A Source of Strength

One reason the means of grace are necessary is that our human nature is such a problem. Though made for God, we are drawn away from God constantly. We have inner conflicts. We have distractions. And we have numberless moods that are alien to the Spirit.

The great principle of the devotional life—confirmed in two thousand years of Christian history—is this: *in returning shall be your strength.* We cannot think of God all the time, but we can return to him again and again daily. Our task here is to punctuate the sentences of each day with thoughts, prayers, and openness to the Holy Spirit.

A general and reliable observation is that those who neglect the means of grace lose the presence and power of the Spirit. Those who cultivate the means of grace tend to be open and receptive to the Spirit's power.

Therefore, we believe it is God's will for us to go to church, to pray, to study the Bible, to memorize key verses, to sing hymns, to share in the sacraments, to seek the deeper meaning of the holy days, and to miss no opportunity to do good. We do not enter upon these activities and carry them through without the help of the Holy Spirit. He reminds us to go to church, to cultivate family religion, to pray for others as well as ourselves, to forgive, to read the Bible, to read constructive materials, books, and articles that build us up, to think and meditate, to give of our means as God has prospered us, and to serve whenever we can.

Openness Versus Forms

We face the danger of allowing these habits of the Christian life to become mere forms. They may be dead routines, lifeless, having the form but not the substance of the Spirit-filled life. This happens whenever the habits of Christian living become the ends rather than the means. If, for instance, we set apart a time for Bible study and prayer as a mere routine, the Spirit departs from us. But if we enter those periods with a sense of expectancy, of new insight, and, above all, of renewed openness to the Holy Spirit, the habit is indeed a *means* of grace. So it is with public worship, the sacrament of the Lord's Supper, unselfish service, and the other means of grace.

11

The Holy Spirit and The Concern for Souls

Our most familiar symbol for Paul is an open Bible with a sword. "Spiritus Gladius" is the Latin for "Sword of the Spirit."

Jesus' Concern

● No one can reflect for long on Jesus' life and teachings and miss his concern for the salvation of souls. He wanted people to have healthy bodies, so he healed them. He wanted the hungry fed, the naked clothed, the sick and imprisoned visited, and the bereaved comforted. But above all, he wanted everyone to enter into the life-giving relationship with God.

When John the Baptist was in prison, he heard about Jesus' deeds and sent word asking, "Are you he who is to come, or shall we look for another?" Jesus answered, "Go and tell John what you hear and see: the blind receive their sight and the lame walk, lepers are cleansed and the deaf hear, and the dead are raised up, and the poor have good news preached to them. And blessed is he who takes no offense at me." (Matthew 11:4-6)

If, from reading this, we get the impression that Jesus

came primarily to minister to the physical needs of people and not their souls, we err greatly. We cannot think of him primarily as a social worker or a physician or as one who saw his mission as merely this-worldly.

His mission was to be the Savior of the world. "For the Son of man came to seek and to save the lost." (Luke 19: 10) John 3:16, which as nearly as any single verse sums up the revealed religion of the Bible, implies this. "For God sent the Son into the world, not to condemn the world, but that the world might be saved through him." (John 3:17) He did not come to judge the world but "to save the world." (12:47) This became a well-known saying among Christians: "The saying is sure and worthy of full acceptance, that Christ came into the world to save sinners." (1 Timothy 1:15)

● Jesus' primary concern was to draw people to God. His mighty deeds were not ends in themselves. They were means to awaken people to God. We read, "Then he began to upbraid the cities where most of his mighty works had been done, because they did not repent, 'Woe to you Chorazin! woe to you Bethsaida! for if the mighty works done in you had been done in Tyre and Sidon, they would have repented long ago in sackcloth and ashes.'" (Matthew 11:20-21) *Of first importance, then, was getting right with God.* And this has to do with the soul's salvation.

Even the account of the last judgment, when the Lord separates the sheep from the goats, concerns the salvation of souls. Two of the key words are *come* and *depart*. Those who were saved were the ones so filled with God's love that they fed the hungry, clothed the naked, visited the sick and imprisoned. The inner condition of their souls as related to God was reflected in their outer ministry to "one of the least of these my brethren," and each of these least ones was identified with Jesus Christ. (Matthew 25:31-46)

So true is all this that if we were to think of Jesus as concerned merely with the this-worldly well-being of people, his unique glory as Lord and Savior would disappear from the horizon. He would be reduced to being another doer of good. More than that, he would be reduced to being just another person who assumed that the answers to one's deepest moral and spiritual needs could be found within the dimensions of this present realm.

We know that Jesus belongs in the unique sphere of the God-man relationships. He felt and taught that each person should be concerned primarily with his soul's salvation and with the salvation of others. In this sphere the true glory of Jesus Christ becomes visible to those with eyes to see. And here his passion for souls is revealed.

This perspective of Jesus stands in marked contrast to certain prevailing assumptions about people in the twentieth century. One of these assumptions has been that a person is essentially a child of nature—not of God. But Jesus and his followers throughout Christian history have seen persons as children of God who exist as creatures in God's physical universe. Body and soul are both important.

The Holy Spirit's Concern for Our Salvation

The Holy Spirit moves in the hearts of persons to seek their own salvation through faith in Christ, and he turns them into evangels. That is, they become concerned to help others know the joys of forgiveness and the glory of the new life in Christ. The Holy Spirit helps them see each human being, including "one of the least"—as Jesus did—as made to move in two realms and not just one. The Holy Spirit illuminates their understanding so that they see beyond a flicker of doubt that everyone needs to be saved. The this-worldly needs of people are to be recognized and ministered to. Jesus saw this clearly. But over and beyond this is *the unique dimension of faith wherein the soul comes to terms with God.*

Every outstanding follower of Jesus has known and felt this. Can anyone imagine Peter or Paul unconcerned about the salvation of souls? Who can read the four Gospels without being keenly aware of the desire of the writers to be evangels?

Similarly, when we read the Acts of the Apostles, we see evidences that the Holy Spirit has given people the passion for the salvation of souls.

Paul as Evangelist

Paul's letters reflect this passion from beginning to end. Even when he wrote to instruct, he did so to help people grow in grace and in the knowledge of God's love in Jesus Christ.

115

In one of the finest statements expressing this passion for souls Paul said: "For though I am free from all men, I have made myself a slave to all, that I might win the more. To the Jews I became as a Jew, in order to win Jews; . . . To those outside the law I became as one outside the law—not being without law toward God but under the law of Christ—that I might win those outside the law. To the weak I became weak, that I might win the weak. I have become all things to all men, that I might by all means save some." (1 Corinthians 9:19-22)

Paul's deepest assumption about people is that whether they are rich or poor, gentile or Jew, male or female, young or old, slave or free, they are made for God, and God is now available through Jesus Christ.

Others With a Passion for Souls

● Augustine, under the power of the same Holy Spirit, was likewise set in motion with this passion for souls. He expended his energies tirelessly in visiting, preaching, and instructing concerning the salvation of souls.

Augustine says that he cannot be surpassed in "desire for a life of unlaborious ease," reading the Bible, thinking, writing. "That is delightful; that is a really good thing. But to preach, to argue, to correct, to try and build up, to strive for individual souls! There you have the real burden, a mighty load, grievous toil. Who would not shrink from it? Yet, again, it is always the Gospel that terrifies me!"[1]

● We need not multiply names of great Christian evangels. A few might be considered, with John Wesley mentioned first. We might think of him as a reformer, a social worker, or even an educator. But when people came out of the coal mines or—what may have been more degrading—their dingy homes, dirty streets, and foul saloons to hear him preach and teach, the one overwhelming impression must have been *that a man of God had come into their midst*. Why? Because they recognized that, above all, he was concerned with the salvation of their souls.

This could be illustrated again and again. But consider one instance: John Wesley wrote an interesting entry in

---

[1] Quoted in *St. Augustine of Hippo*, by Hugh Pope (Image Books Edition 1961 by special arrangement with Newman Press), p 138. Used by permission of Paulist Press.

his *Journal* on Wednesday, February 28, 1787. He was eighty-four years old. And what was his obvious passion? Let his own words express it: "We went over to Plymouth, and found the Society doubled since I was here before; and they are both more loving than they were then, and more earnest to save their souls."[2] He did not say that they had developed a passion to make resolutions on the state of the nation or to get some community project going. He said that they were "more earnest to save their souls." Out of this deep spirituality came the planned programs of service to those in need. Thus, again, the Holy Spirit, who always seeks to magnify Jesus Christ in the world, enabled John Wesley to experience and express this passion for souls.

● Another early leader with this evangelical passion for souls was Philip William Otterbein. In 1751 in Herborn, Germany, he answered the call of Michael Schlatter for missionaries with certain qualities to go to America. Otterbein had those qualities: "orthodox, learned, pious and of humble disposition, diligent, sound in body and eagerly desirous not after earthly but heavenly treasure, especially the salvation of immortal souls."[3]

Two other early United Methodist leaders who had a passion for souls were Martin Boehm and Jacob Albright. Both of these men probably died prematurely because of their extensive travels over mountainous territory preaching the urgency of salvation.[4]

The Holy Spirit and Our Witness

● In keeping with this evangelical passion, the Holy Spirit helps Christians see clearly the simple but life-shaking processes people must undergo to be saved. They must feel the pangs of remorse and failure. They must repent. They must have faith. They must be eager for and open to God's love in Christ. They must immediately look for opportunities for helping others and lose no occasion for doing good.

The Holy Spirit helps us get across to others the im-

---

[2] *The Journal of John Wesley*, IV, p. 369.
[3] From *These Evangelical United Brethren*, by Paul H. Eller (Abingdon Press, 1957), p. 24. Out of print.
[4] *Ibid.*, pp. 26-31.

portance and power of faith. Christian faith is unique. Only through it can the processes of salvation be set in motion. Even repentance presupposes some faith. Who would confess his sins if he did not trust in a forgiving God?

The Holy Spirit helps us awaken in others this trust in God as he is manifested in Jesus Christ. In this way the soul passes from "death" to life. It is carried into that new dimension of existence by virtue of this new relationship with God. But people need help from others to have faith. Therefore, the Spirit works through our spirits to help others experience a new faith, a new glory, and a new sense of the mystery and joy of living. People need help from others to know that God loves them, that they are claimed by God and called to the life of adventuring with God in creative living.

The Holy Spirit, then, does not send people out merely with the passion to evangelize. He increases their understanding so that they can help others to know how they can be saved and to lead them into fellowship with God. He enables them to see that in the unique sphere of the religious the way is opened to persons by the Christ who is the Way.

The Holy Spirit helps us see also that souls are neither saved nor nurtured in the Christian life apart from the community of faith. The Bible, so essential here, *is* the church's book. God speaks through the living Word. This means that Christians must get together for worship, praise, prayer, Bible study, spiritual support, and service.

● The Holy Spirit works also in Christians to help them find improved ways, whether old or new, of winning people to Jesus Christ. Evangelism is no simple process. Dealing with the souls of persons is difficult. It requires resourcefulness, wisdom, patience, prayer, helpfulness. Often a first step is to get people interested in joining a group within a local church that is doing something worthwhile for the Lord. This means that, prior to drawing people in, we must have something to offer through the community of faith. No one is likely to be won to Christ by people who are not involved in meaningful activities in and through the church.

The main purpose here is not to suggest ways of evangelizing—though that is of utmost importance—but to show that the Holy Spirit wants us by all commendable means to woo people into the new life in Christ. As Paul put it: ". . . that I might by all means save some." (1 Corinthians 9:22) Evangelism, in its inner spirit, is the permanent disposition to persuade people to open their lives to God. This disposition or passion is born and nurtured by the Holy Spirit. It is carried out not merely through individuals but through the total effort of all those who are joined together in the community of faith.

● Some people have difficulty in witnessing. Some are ashamed to bear witness. The Holy Spirit overcomes that through the help of others in the community of faith. Some are timid and feel that they cannot do it. The Holy Spirit overcomes that, too. Some are so busy with other "good" activities that they fail to concentrate on this primary ministry of all Christians. The Holy Spirit helps us here also by working in and through the whole fellowship of believers.

The Holy Spirit will not let us forget that God wants to draw all people to himself. He wants them to put their trust in him and to belong to him. Jesus said, "Truly, I say to you, unless you turn and become like children, you will never enter the kingdom of heaven" (Matthew 18:3), for we receive the Kingdom, like a child, in simple faith. When Jesus taught us to pray to God as Father, he taught us to feel toward him as the "dear Father" that a little child feels in a good home. The Holy Spirit moves in us to help all to feel and pray, "Dear Father." This too becomes real within the community of faith.

12

The Holy Spirit and Responsible Living In Community

We have seen that God is dynamic, active. He is moving toward the realization of goals. His concern for human beings is that they grow in attaining worthy aims. He seeks always to help them in this process. Therefore, a primary mission of the Holy Spirit is to move within us to realize worthy goals on earth.

From Inner Power to Honest Deeds

Some imagine that the Spirit's concern is simply to give us inner joy and peace without regard to the achievement of aims. But God is concerned both with the inner soul and the outer deeds that flow from it. In fact, the true understanding of divine grace is that it strives and stirs mysteriously within us to produce good deeds here and now. Inner grace and outer deeds are joined together by the Holy Spirit, and what God has joined together let not man put asunder.

One of John Wesley's most important contributions to vital religion was the special way in which he tied together the inner experience of God's presence with the outer conduct that necessarily flows from it. Wesley never weakened in stressing the new inner life of the soul produced by the transforming presence of the Holy Spirit. At the same time, he always connected this with good works, for faith is "completed by works." (James 2:22)

In August, 1738, when Wesley was visiting the Moravian Church in Germany, he received detailed reports on that evangelical movement. He included in his *Journal* an account of that movement by one of their members, Christian David. Mr. David reported that back in 1732 the church at Herrnhut had deplored the laxity of life, even among Lutherans and Calvinists, for these too were insisting so much on faith as to forget "holiness and good works." He reported further, "Observing this terrible abuse of preaching Christ *given for us,* we began to insist more than ever on Christ *living in us.*"

This is basic, for what we experience inwardly and what we do outwardly go together.

The Christian experience of the Holy Spirit is directly connected with the Christian moral life. Morality has to do with how we act, or with what we do. Christian morality has to do with the *conduct* of people who are transformed by the Holy Spirit. The inner quality of soul—though involving inner peace, assurance, and joy in the Lord—*aims toward practical results, or action, for good.* Therefore, the Christian, under the influence of the Holy Spirit, expresses what might be called the *morality of results.* He wants the well-being for people which is to be obtained only through good works. God realizes his kingdom in us and through us.

---

[1] *Journal*, II, 35.

Another way of describing the morality that flows from the presence of the Holy Spirit is to call it *Christian purposive morality,* for it seeks good. Just as God seeks his best for all people, so those who receive the power of the Holy Spirit are *programed toward human good* on earth.

Basic Errors

Against this background we see clearly two basic errors regarding the power and presence of the Holy Spirit.

One is that the Holy Spirit affects the inner life and is not much concerned with outer deeds. The other error is that the Holy Spirit has to do with social action and does not care much about inner spirituality. The former leads to quietness, private devotions, inner tranquility. As we have seen, these are very important. But inner rightness disconnected from outer deeds is a mockery of vital Christianity. And the stress on social action without any real concern for those inner dynamic processes from which the deeds flow is as phony as it is unchristian.

We need to carry these thoughts further. Some people imagine that their Christian duties are confined to personal services to individuals in need without regard to the larger influences in society and in nations. When we reflect on these matters, we see that the Christian is called of God both to minister to the needs of individuals and to exert responsible leadership in the community as a whole. Why? Because the souls of people and their bodies are profoundly helped or harmed by the quality of the societies in which they live and work.

● Unfortunately, the *tradition of passivity* spreads like a wet blanket over the church. By "tradition of passivity" I mean the belief, handed down from generation to generation, that we cannot or need not or should not do anything about the larger affairs of community life.

Those who say that we *cannot do anything* about them are either fatalists or predestinarians, and in either case that these matters are beyond our control. In other words, they adopt a do-nothing attitude.

Those who say that we *need not do anything* about these larger affairs believe that God will work everything out regardless of what we do.

Those who say that we *should not* do anything about the

123

larger affairs assume that otherwise we would be tampering with God's prerogatives. Thus, out of a kind of false piety they do not hear the Spirit's summons to responsible living in community.

Sometimes the difference is not clear between serving individuals and acting responsibly *in relation to the larger forces of society*. But most of the time we can recognize a difference. Much has been written about the fall of the Roman Empire, but that was vastly different from the fall of a Roman citizen. Personal concerns and individual needs are very important, but we must not overlook or ignore those larger forces that affect the fate and fortune of vast multitudes of persons.

● The issue here is one of the most crucial for the community of faith. As Christians under the power of the Holy Spirit, are we summoned to do our best to redirect the larger forces of society? To raise the question seriously is to answer it, for Jesus taught us to pray,

> "Thy kingdom come,
> They will be done,
> On earth as it is in heaven."
> (Matthew 6:10)

What are these larger forces? They are the cultural, political, economic, institutional, and moral influences on the lives of large numbers of people in a community. The larger forces and larger affairs have to do with social patterns, structures, and institutions that affect humankind.

Augustine, Luther, and Wesley

The biblical revelation has been interpreted by some in a way that leaves the larger social forces outside the reach of the gospel and of Christian responsibility.

Christianity, it has been said, concerns the salvation of souls, comfort and encouragement, and the life everlasting. Augustine, for all of his greatness, expressed this view again and again in his *City of God*.

Martin Luther, though exerting wide influences on the larger affairs of his day, wrote repeatedly that Christians were to leave alone the larger affairs of the political and economic orders. They were to accept conditions as they were and submit to the powers that existed.

One factor that influenced Luther's passivity was his belief that the end of the world was at hand—the Lord would soon return. Therefore, people need not try to change institutions, political forces, and the like.

Again and again, we hear the cries: "Let the church be the church." "Stay out of politics and economics." "Stick to your task of saving souls."

A part of John Wesley's genius was that he knew that Christians were called through the Holy Spirit to act responsibly in community. He opposed slavery and condemned as unchristian the buying and selling of human beings as slaves. With him the grace of God was always tied to action. For him that meant that Christians were moved to improve *the context* in which life is lived. He and his teams of workers went into the prisons to preach, teach, and bring needed clothes, food, and bedding to the prisoners. He assisted people in getting jobs and gave them useful materials to read. *Wesley did not allow the work of the Holy Spirit in persons to be disconnected from responsible living in community.* United Methodists today, from both the German and English traditions, have their motive and being in the line of Wesley, Albright, and Otterbein.

The Spirit and Social Change

● The Holy Spirit seeks to effect changes in society through people. The Holy Spirit is necessarily concerned with *ways and means* of doing this which reflect the spirit of Jesus Christ. No matter how Christian the goal may be, if the means are destructive and dishonorable, the Holy Spirit is not governing the action. The means used often repudiate the ends desired. For this reason the community of faith is opposed to violent methods. As Jesus said: "All who take the sword will perish by the sword." (Matthew 26:52) We see nothing in our Christian summons to responsible leadership in community affairs which involves social chaos or anarchy.

Social change is inevitable and may be for better or worse. The community of faith, when led by the Spirit, seeks constructive changes in society. Changes may be brought about through normal or unusual ways. One of the surest signs of the presence of the Holy Spirit in these processes is the evidence of orderly progress. For this reason I have used the word *responsible*. This implies practical good sense, a grasp of the relevant facts, patience in working with people, and persistence and resourcefulness in moving toward the God-appointed goals.

● The importance of this view becomes self-evident when we consider what is taking place in the world.

Look at political affairs. Does not the Holy Spirit move in us to encourage and promote honesty in politics? Is this not a Christian duty in every era?

Consider alcoholism and drug addiction. Here we are dealing with vast forces—economic, political, educational, moral—which affect millions of people. Is it right for any Christian or community of Christians to ignore these and other ancient and profit-making social evils? The Holy Spirit continues to summon us to leadership in overcoming these demonic forces.

What about marriage and the family order? Are we as Christians to scamper for shelter and not confront the moral sickness that leads people to repudiate the validity and sanctity of marriage? Are we to ignore the tendencies to belittle the authority of parents and teachers?

What about war and peace? Are these matters to be left to political leaders without constant efforts for peace on the part of Christian people? Are not the political leaders themselves to be open to the movement of the Spirit? Beyond reasonable doubt many young people throughout the United States through their persistent efforts toward peace in Vietnam influenced political leaders to act for peace. The Christian mind and heart is committed to peace. The Council of Bishops of The United Methodist Church has rightly joined other Christian leaders in calling upon the community of faith to work together toward "peace and the self-development of peoples" throughout the world. The Holy Spirit works in people toward national and international peace with justice.

Among the most serious problems of the world as we look toward the twenty-first century is that of racial prejudice. Surely the Holy Spirit moves in our hearts to enable us to experience full mutual respect toward *all* people. The Spirit summons us to act accordingly. Persons of all races are equally precious in the Father's sight, and Christ lived and died for all.

What about other issues, such as pollution, overpopulation, organized crime, pornography, the tragic aspects of abuse of the mass media? Are these of no concern to God? On the contrary, the Holy Spirit moves within people in the community of faith to act responsibly in these large affairs.

● An implication of the gospel is that we should reflect on these social issues so that we may bring our minds, transformed by the Holy Spirit, to bear on them. The gospel implies also that Christians should be present in body and mind in the decision-making processes relative to these problems. By implication also this places upon many people special obligations as Christians who, by virtue of their office or position in society, can exert leadership under the guidance of the Holy Spirit.

These views are implied in the biblical teaching on God, our Father, who always seeks the best for *all* his children. We find also the biblical teaching that God works through people to do good. Hence, the call comes to us to responsible leadership. The great characters of the Bible often took the leadership in community affairs, and the Christian ethic of love requires this. The Holy Spirit enables us to work with God for the realization of his Kingdom on earth as far as possible.

The Holy Spirit and The Ecumenical Spirit

This symbol for the World Council of Churches includes a ship's mast in the form of a cross and the Greek word meaning the universality of the church and its worldwide mission.

Christians of all denominations remember Jesus' prayer for the unity of his followers. He prayed that his disciples might be one. (John 17:11) In anticipation, he prayed for all those who were to believe on him through the apostles, that they too might be one. (17:20-21) The Holy Spirit has been concerned to answer that prayer.

One sure sign of the presence of the Holy Spirit is the deep-seated love that Christians have for one another. The yearning to join hands with fellow Christians around the world is the work of the Holy Spirit in the hearts of believers. The contemporary desire for Christian unity is in its essence a manifestation of the Holy Spirit.

Current Ecumenical Efforts

In spite of all the ecumenical efforts of the twentieth century, the results have been in large measure disappointing. Some of the most devoted champions of Christian unity on the contemporary scene feel disillusioned over the prospects. Vatican Council II, under the amiable leadership of Pope John XXIII, seemed to some to hold great promise for ecumenism. Conversations have been going on among Roman Catholics and representatives of nearly every other major Christian body.

Good has been accomplished. The points of agreement and of difference have been clearly identified. But we have seen very few signs of any willingness to make major changes on the issues that separate Christians. *They do not even agree on open communion around the Lord's Table.*

The primary issue in the disagreements concerns the interpretation of apostolic succession. Certain groups refuse to recognize fully the ordained ministry of other churches even when the standards for ordination are very high. They say, in effect, "Oh yes, we recognize you as authentic clergymen, but on a lower level." Various theological and historical claims are made to justify this ecclesiastical point of view. But none of these claims has an authentic ring in the light of the total spirit and teaching of Jesus.

Other large groups of Christians isolate themselves from their fellow Christians and refuse to join in conversations on issues of major importance on the contemporary scene.

A few Christian churches with common heritages have united. Others are talking about union. Important gains have been made in numberless local communities where Christians have united to support special projects of various kinds. But, generally speaking, the results so far have been disappointing and even frustrating.

● Why have so many efforts toward ecumenism failed to take Christians further along the way toward unity?

Thoughtful people will differ in their responses to this question.

Some persons will say that not enough leadership was shown at the grass roots level. Outstanding experts who have made careers of ecumenism have done their work well, but a great gulf has separated them from the masses of Christians. The aims of the Holy Spirit have been blocked by the failure to build bridges across the gulfs that separate the ecumenical experts from the multitudes.

Others would say that the failure to move steadily toward Christian unity was caused by artificial elements in the proposed plans of union. People sat down together, talked, wrote papers, and came up with plans that pieced together several characteristics of the participating groups. But somehow the plans seemed more concocted than real. Some gains have been made here, however. Among these, the best, perhaps, is in the *improved theological or doctrinal statements.*

Some of these gains in doctrinal unity are surely manifestations of the Holy Spirit, but much else is as artificial as it is impractical. Most people at the grass roots have found it hard to give a positive response to some of the proposed plans for church union. Yet the recognition of alternatives that will not work is a significant step.

A third obstacle is related to the ones discussed above. Some persons have said that the passion for church union may have obscured the need for diversity among Christians. T. S. Eliot said that "no culture has appeared or developed except together with a religion." He went on to say that one of three important conditions of culture "is the balance of unity and diversity in religion—that is, universality of doctrine with particularity of cult and devotion."[1] *The Holy Spirit does not seem concerned to stifle diversity in Christianity. But he seems to be forever seeking unity amid and through diversity.*

Other factors standing in the way of Christian unity have more to do with pride and prejudice than with errors of judgment. Man's sinfulness, even in the churches, has been a major obstacle to the Holy Spirit's concern for unity. Pride of church, racial prejudice, stubborn adherence to old thoughts and ways without sufficient regard for the directives of revealed religion, fear of change, the sinful nurture of historical cleavages—these and other sins have kept Christians apart.

Why Not a Federation of Christians?

Perhaps the approach of E. Stanley Jones and some others toward a federation of Christians may more nearly

---

[1] From *Christianity and Culture*, by T. S. Eliot (Harcourt, Brace and Company, Harvest Book, 1949), pp. 87-88.

express the leadership of the Holy Spirit than any other efforts of the present century.

Some possible guidelines for discussion may be suggested.

● First, instead of beginning with the emphasis on union or even on federation, perhaps we should start with the clear built-in guarantee of the distinctiveness and identity of each participating member. This calls for loyalty to and understanding of one's own communion. This implies also a built-in commitment to mutual appreciation and respect. It further implies, as a matter of policy, a determination from the start to oppose the demonic passion for monolithic domination over even the smallest groups.

In our own case, for example, this commitment would include remembering to say *United* Methodist Church in conversation. It also would mean the updating of signs on our church buildings to reflect the inclusion of former separate bodies into our united church. Furthermore, it would mean including illustrations from the many branches and roots of our former denominations when discussing our history or heritage. Such references are not merely a perpetuation of relics of the past, but a genuine recognition of the meaning and significance of that which each of us brought into union.

● Second, all groups should develop a growing appreciation for the distinctive leaders, events, and doctrinal emphases that have made the several communions what they now are. In this way all threats of disintegration, or loss of identity, of Christian groups would be removed. The curious notion that any denomination should lose itself so that a larger unity might follow would be discarded as impractical, for what we seem to require is unity-in-variety.

● Third, cooperative efforts should be made to identify those areas and issues where joint study, prayer, and action would benefit not only all Christians but all the sinful, pagan, and secular world as well. These should be large areas that have to do with the survival of Christianity as a vital religion and also with the tragic moral and spiritual conditions in the world.

Perhaps such a federation would have regular times of meeting on a massive scale—say once every ten years. Or, when necessary, they could meet on call. On those occasions—preceded by the most careful preparation—Christians could join forces in making sound assessments of humankind's condition. They could share in making credible statements of purpose and policy. They could join forces in world evangelization.

● Fourth, these guidelines imply the steadfast refusal to get bogged down in petty bickering over what may seem to be primary issues but which always get reduced to the lower levels of cheap criticism. At this point I know of no nobler guideline outside the Bible than that of John Wesley's sermon on the catholic spirit. He said that even among Christians "it must needs be, that, as long as there are various opinions, there will be various ways of worshipping God; seeing a variety of opinions necessarily implies a variety of practice."[2] Wesley said he would not ask everyone to go to the church he himself preferred or to worship in the same way he did or to believe in and administer the sacraments as he did or to accept the form of church government he liked best. Then he added: "Let all these things stand by: we will talk of them, if need be, at a more convenient season; my only question at present is this, 'Is thine heart right, as my heart is with thy heart?' "[3]

● A fifth guideline is implied in the others, namely, that all who assume roles of leadership in ecumenism should have doctrinal and historical competence on the one hand and extraordinary powers of negotiation and boundless patience on the other. Here too the power of the Holy Spirit is necessary.

The Supreme Aim of Ecumenism

In and through everything, the Holy Spirit's summons to magnify Jesus Christ and his kingdom is paramount.

● As we move rapidly toward the twenty-first century, we begin to see that at least three primary factors are at work which challenge all Christians.

One is the *threat of secularity* that obscures the relevance of religion in general and Christianity in particular. Here the need is to study, reflect, pray, and join forces even as we maintain our own distinctive heritages.

---

[2] *Standard Sermons*, II, 133.
[3] *Standard Sermons*, II, 136.

A second factor concerns the encounter with other world religions and the various sects stemming from them. Christianity is a *world* religion. We cannot avoid what hopefully may become creative encounters with other religious groups. Moreover, in nearly all nations we find smaller sect groups with roots in non-Christian religions. Every era has its *gurus,* or self-appointed "spiritual leaders." Here, too, joint efforts among Christians will prove to be most beneficial to all.

A third factor—complex and devastating—which calls for united efforts is the breakdown of authority and the consequent moral decay of people during these last decades of the twentieth century. This is a disaster of the most awesome proportions imaginable. No other tragedy on the contemporary scene compares with it in magnitude and consequence. Obviously the Holy Spirit is calling upon Christians to unite for the moral and spiritual transformation of people throughout the world. Nothing short of the renewing power of the Holy Spirit is equal to the task.

● Such a federation as here suggested might be fairly loose. But these large areas of crucial need would require the will to join hands and to share in study, prayer, proclamation, work, and service in every community and throughout the whole world. In some such ways, through the mysterious movement of the Holy Spirit, our Lord's prayer for unity might be answered more fully than ever before.

THE HOLY SPIRIT
AND THE
CHARISMATIC
MOVEMENT

The Holy Spirit and Speaking in Tongues

The practice of speaking in tongues (glossolalia—glos-o-la'-le-a) occurred in certain churches during the first two and a half centuries of the Christian era—until around A.D. 250. Then it disappeared almost entirely during the next fourteen centuries—from 250 until around 1650. It recurred at intervals from that time until 1900 when it began to manifest itself more extensively than ever before.

The pentecostal movement in the United States is considered to have begun about 1900. During the past two decades the movement known as neopentecostalism ("new" pentecostalism) has appeared in many of the mainline churches.

Among Non-Christians

Speaking in unknown tongues has not been confined to Christianity. Similar practices have been reported among people of various religions and cultures before Christ. For example, Herodotus, the ancient Greek historian who has been called the father of history, reported on a ceremony in the cult of Isis (Egyptian). He said that the people reached a state of frenzy, inflicted wounds upon themselves, and uttered unintelligible sounds. Though that was vastly different from Christians speaking in tongues, it was at least similar in that utterances of no known language poured from the mouths of those involved. Speaking, or "prophesying," in unintelligible sounds was known to some extent also among the Canaanites, Israelites, Arabs, and Greeks. It occurred in the ancient Greek mystery religions where, through a series of ceremonial stages, the devotees were led to states of ecstasy and spoke languages known only to one another. Instances could be multiplied also from studies of religious practices around the world.[1]

Montanus and Montanism

Returning now to Christian history, we recall that some of the early believers at Corinth and Ephesus spoke in unknown tongues. Various studies have revealed also that speaking in tongues was practiced among Christians in Phrygia (in Asia Minor) during the second and third centuries. This was particularly notable under the influence of Montanus, a Phrygian who flourished during the latter part of the second century.

Christians may have spoken in tongues in many local churches of which we have no record. Irenaeus (130?-200), who did his work as a great Christian theologian and defender of the faith during the second half of the second century, seems to have had firsthand knowledge of Christians speaking in tongues. He observed that though he himself did not speak in tongues, many others did. E. Glenn Hinson, basing his conclusion on important studies of Heinrich Weinel (1899) and others, says: "In the second and early third centuries . . . the evidences for glossolalia apart from Montanism are substantial." [2] Nevertheless, the early church fathers made very few references to it.

---

[1] See "Glossolalia in Historical Perspective," by John T. Bunn, in *Speaking in Tongues: Let's Talk About It,* Watson E. Mills, ed. (Word Books, 1973), pp. 36-47.

[2] *Ibid,* pp. 64-65.

A few more remarks, however, about Montanus may be helpful in this context. His primary emphasis was not on speaking in tongues but on the illuminating work of the Holy Spirit. The early church historian Eusebius said of Montanus that he would be overcome by a sudden seizure, fall into a trance and speak in unknown tongues. Montanus is said to have had his first such experience around 156. His followers believed that the Holy Spirit was specially revealed in him. Montanism as a movement spread to North Africa and was given considerable impetus when Tertullian (160?-230?) of Carthage became a Montanist around 200, for he was one of the outstanding writers of the early church.

Montanists were opposed from the start by many church leaders. But the opposition to them was not based primarily on the fact that they spoke in tongues. Some said that they were too fond of taking up collections. Also, the Montanists believed that women should be given the right to perform all functions of the church. However, no one could charge them validly with moral laxity, for they were strongly ascetic and rigorous in their demands upon their adherents. They wanted a return to vital Christianity.

The real opposition to Montanism came from the conviction of the church that this movement was not built essentially on Jesus and the apostles. The Montanists believed in the revelation that began in the religion of Israel and which was continued through Christ and the apostles. But they believed also that the Holy Spirit carried that revelation into a new dispensation through Montanus. They held that a new era of prophecy was begun which was far more than a mere extension of Pentecost. They claimed that the Spirit spoke in *new* revelations through the ecstatic experiences and "prophecies" of Montanus. He emphasized the idea that people became passive organs of the Spirit who manifested himself in visions and ecstatic experiences.

After many years of discussion, debate, denunciation, Montanism was officially repudiated by the church in the fourth century.

Virtual Disappearance of Speaking in Tongues

In general, the evidence for the practice of speaking in tongues among early Christians after 250 is almost non-

139

existent. By the fourth century it was virtually unknown both to Chrysostom (345?-407) in the Greek community and to Augustine (354-430) in the Latin community. They tended to assume that the gift of tongues served as a sign in the earliest days of Christianity but was no longer useful.

Even the Middle Ages, when people tended to believe readily in the occult and the supernatural, left almost no evidence of speaking in unknown tongues. Since then, scattered groups in the seventeenth and eighteenth centuries, including the Jansenists (a Catholic holiness order), Quakers, Shakers, and others claimed the gift of tongues. But they did not make it a central feature of their experience.

Among Early Methodists

Though the early Methodists emphasized the power of the Holy Spirit, they did not make a practice of speaking in tongues. This must be made clear because some have associated John Wesley and his followers with this kind of pentecostalism. Wesley did not belittle those who claimed the gift of tongues. On scriptural grounds he tended to respect the Spirit's unusual gifts, including the gift of tongues.[3] He denied that he had this gift of speaking in what he called "new tongues." When he was charged with claiming in his journals that he had extraordinary gifts of the Spirit, he replied by saying, "You do not know that in these very Journals I utterly disclaim the 'extraordinary gifts of the Spirit,' and all other 'influences and operations of the Holy Ghost' than those that are common to all real Christians." [4]

Wesley knew from observation, as Paul did from experience, that the claims to such charismatic gifts of the Spirit as speaking in tongues did not necessarily help people love one another and serve their fellow human beings.

In Wesley's *Notes Upon the New Testament* he said very little about Paul's remarks on speaking in tongues. What he did not say is as important as what he said. For example, regarding Paul's statement, "I thank God that I speak in tongues more than you all" (1 Corinthians 14:18), Wesley

---

[3] *Letters*, II, 363-65.
[4] *Letters*, IV, 327; also 340-41.

made no comment whatever. Why? Because he believed this served no useful purpose to his readers. Why not? Because Wesley was interested primarily in the righteousness-producing practical activity of the Holy Spirit which is available to all. He shared deeply in what Paul was really after, namely, the life so filled with the Spirit as to express Christ's love.

The Pentecostal Movement in the United States

● During the present century the pentecostal movement in the United States, which encompasses far more than speaking in tongues, has been an extension of the holiness movement. It has become visible in the Assemblies of God in Christ, the various Churches of God, and other similar groups.

One variety of holiness groups has stressed sanctification as a second definite work of grace without much specific emphasis on special gifts of the Holy Spirit, such as speaking in unknown tongues. The other variety of holiness groups—here referred to as the pentecostal groups—has stressed "baptism in the Spirit," with a strong emphasis on speaking in tongues as a sign and a witness and on other special, or charismatic, gifts such as healing, prophecy, and exorcism of evil spirits.

The pentecostal groups tended to be hostile toward higher education and theological education for ministers. *The Holy Spirit, it was believed, would instantly inspire the ministers and other leaders on what to say and do.* Hence, academic studies were not needed. Indeed, these

141

were often thought of as interfering with the free movement of the Spirit. This view necessarily put a wall of separation between the pentecostal groups and the mainline churches. Another divisive factor was the insistence by many persons that speaking in tongues was *a necessary sign of baptism in the Spirit*. Many divisive forces in the pentecostal movement led to the formation of various sects, from those emphasizing healing and exorcism (expelling evil spirits) to those specializing in snake handling.

● Nevertheless, the pentecostal movement as a whole, despite its diversities, is a major force within contemporary Christendom. Approximately two million Christians in the United States are members of pentecostal churches where speaking in tongues is practiced. Because of the missionary outreach of many of them, the movement has become worldwide. We should note in passing, however, that many of those Christian groups who started out emphasizing the gift of tongues and other special gifts have not continued to make this a primary feature of their life and practice.

The Emergence of Neopentecostalism

The charismatic movement, which emphasizes special gifts, has come to visibility more recently in so-called neopentecostalism, which is pentecostalism within the traditional churches. This is a movement of small groups, within the Roman Catholic and Protestant churches, which share in pentecostal experiences.

As is well known, these groups emphasize "baptism in the Spirit" and the consequent charismatic, or "special," gifts of the Spirit. In addition to the primary Christian virtues—faith, hope, and love—they insist that those who experience "baptism in the Spirit" are endowed by the Holy Spirit with special gifts of speaking in unknown tongues, of healing, of discernment, and of power to recognize and exorcise demons.

Within the mainline historic Christian churches there are significant modifications in the movement. For example, the neopentecostals do not insist on speaking in tongues as a required proof of "baptism in the Spirit." They are not anti-intellectual. Nor are they suspicious of doctors and medical care. They are not antichurch, and, for the most part, they find their places not only in their smaller pentecostal groups but also within the larger life of the churches to which they belong. Many of the neopentecostals are well educated and well-to-do.

● What does this "baptism in the Spirit" do for the neopentecostals? Or, what does it mean to them?

The answer to these questions is perhaps best seen in private and group prayer. Many neopentecostals, following the guidelines of Scripture, speak in tongues during periods of private prayer. They do not want to make a spectacle of themselves or of this experience. When interviewed, they prefer to remain anonymous.

The group prayer meetings are a central feature of the neopentecostal movement. These vary from place to place and time to time. They may be held in churches or in private homes. They tend to be informal. Yet usually certain persons take the lead. Prayer, reading from the Bible, teaching, hymn singing, silence, and testimony may enter into these meetings. Some have said that speaking in unknown tongues is "prayer language," for God puts the language into people and they respond by speaking it. Sometimes all in the group will pray at the same time, in known or unknown tongues. Special needs may be mentioned, and the group may engage in intercessory prayer. The laying on of hands for the gift of tongues and for healing may also be a part of these prayer meetings.

To those who experience the gift of tongues, whether in private or in small groups, it is a way of expressing joy, adoration, and praise. At its best, it assists them to glorify Christ. They experience a certain transforming power through this act of praise. Also they have a feeling of a closer fellowship with God through "prayer language." The feeling that God has given it puts in them a sense of assurance of God's special favor. "Baptism in the Spirit" is a new work of grace, bringing inner peace and new life. In most cases this takes place instantly, at a definite moment. Some insist that there is no need to tarry, to pray, to go through a long program of study or meditation; it happens suddenly. Others recognize gradual processes leading up to it.

● The neopentecostals claim that this experience marks a new beginning with God. Often it means a moral transformation along with *a new sense of the presence of God.* Neopentecostals feel that they have found a new life in Christ, and they glorify God in the mysterious language of the Spirit. They do not profess to understand all this. They experience it with joy and gratitude. They are the passive recipients of a gift that requires no human skills.

Neopentecostals have the desire to serve God through these charismatic gifts. This is really the heart of the matter for most of them. *They are concerned about the experience of God's presence and power.* With most of them the real issue does not have to do with speaking or not speaking in tongues. The real issue concerns whether or not people experience *the fullness of life in the Holy Spirit from whom the gifts come.*

● Pentecostals and neopentecostals alike insist that their experiences of receiving the charismatic gifts can be understood only through the Spirit. Their experiences admit of psychological analysis, but they cannot be appreciated merely as psychological processes. Psychic forces are at work here, but far more than psychic phenomena are involved. The pentecostals like to quote Paul's reminder that "the unspiritual man does not receive the gifts of the Spirit of God, for they are folly to him, and he is not able to understand them because they are spiritually discerned." (1 Corinthians 2:14)

Some Problems

Without belittling those who have received the genuine gift of tongues, we observe that it has in fact led to division and strife in many local churches. This is because of a judgmental attitude on all sides which makes for divisiveness. Some feel that those who do not have this gift are second-class Christians. This self-righteous attitude reveals that the Holy Spirit has not done his *primary* work in people.

Another unfortunate aspect has been the practice of encouraging *everyone* to speak in tongues, although *God does not give such special gifts to everyone.* (1 Corinthians 12:28-30) This has led to many problems. The neopentecostals have recognized wisely that only "the higher gifts" are for all Christians. (12:31) They have known too that fake and fraud become conspicuous when people offer to show others how to speak in tongues—sometimes on the promise or expectation of a fee. They are particularly aware of the danger of becoming so fascinated with the gift as to forget the Giver and the deeds he expects of all who receive his gifts.

Their claim is that the gift of tongues may be very important and useful to some Christians but that it is not a necessary sign of the presence of the Holy Spirit. For all Christians the indispensable signs of "baptism in the Spirit" are the experienced love of Christ in their hearts and the good deeds that flow from it.

The Church's Response To Speaking In Tongues

The nine points of the star represent the fruits of
the Spirit named in Galatians 5:22. The letters are
the initials of the Latin words for love, joy, peace,
patience, kindness, goodness, faithfulness, gentleness, self-control.

One of the best books on the neopentecostal movement
in the churches is *The Work of the Holy Spirit* (see page
176). This book is significant for several reasons: (1) It
came out of a two-year study (1968-70) by a committee
authorized by a particular community of faith (The United
Presbyterian Church in the United States of America). (2)
It is based on a careful study of Scripture. (3) It presents
essential facts about the contemporary charismatic movement. (4) It is balanced and, because of that, tends to
create mutual understanding and cooperation amid differences. (5) It contains superior evaluations of "baptism
with the Spirit" and of speaking in tongues.

That book symbolizes the way we should go about evaluating what is happening in the churches. The process of evaluation in pratical matters should be done by the church itself. Individuals may have their say. Scholars who have an interest in glossolalia and the charismatic movement render a service by their books and articles. But on a matter of this kind *the whole church, both at the local and general level,* needs to evaluate.

Sometimes our ministers set themselves up as judges on these matters and overlook or neglect the opinions of lay persons. Sometimes the laity wants to evaluate without benefit of the clergy. This too is a mistake. Some would rather not bother to think on these matters at all. This is the easy way out.

The wisest course would seem to be, as the need arises, to give each congregation the opportunity of reflecting prayerfully in study groups for the mutual benefit of all the members. When we are dealing with any issue that bears directly on the activity of the Holy Spirit within the church, the community of faith as a whole—both locally and generally—would want to work together prayerfully and thoughtfully on it.

The community of faith is not left without guidelines and criteria. No particular local church should decide either on these or on any other matters without being aware of that church group as a *historic* community of faith.

Guides for Evaluation

What then are the criteria for evaluating any movement within the church? *The Book of Discipline of The United Methodist Church* gives four bases for evaluating beliefs and practices: (1) Scripture, (2) tradition, (3) experience, and (4) reason. These standards, approved almost unanimously by the General Conference of 1972, came out of a four-year study by a commission on doctrine and doctrinal standards. Of these four, Scripture is the *primary source and guide* for Christian belief and practice. With this in mind, all four standards may commend themselves to thoughtful Christians everywhere.

As we evaluate the practice of speaking in tongues, let us reflect together in keeping with the spirit of these standards and see where we come out. This is the procedure I shall attempt to follow. Each local church might do this also in its own way. This procedure might prove especially helpful in those churches that have division and bad feeling over the practice of speaking in tongues.

Against this background we may ask three questions: How does speaking in tongues stand up in the light of the Bible? How does it stand up in the light of our Christian heritage (tradition)? How does it stand up in the light of practical Christian living? I am including in this last question the established principles of Christian experience and the values of reason and common sense. To these we now turn in that order.

In the Light of the Bible

The neopentecostals affirm that their emphasis on "baptism with the Spirit" and speaking in tongues is based on the Bible. John the Baptist said of Jesus that he would "baptize with the Holy Spirit." (John 1:33; see also Acts 1:5; 11:16.) Jesus promised the power and presence of the Holy Spirit. (John 14:15-17) Moreover, those who speak in tongues insist that this was a special gift of the Spirit ordained of God for Christians. (1 Corinthians 12:28; 14:21) It is a sign of baptism with the Spirit. (Acts 10:45-46; 19:6) Speaking in tongues is a gift for self-edification (1 Corinthians 14:4) and for private communion with God (14:2).

● Let us now consider *the New Testament teaching as a whole*. We may begin by observing that the New Testament was prepared for by the Old. The Old Testament writers knew very little of the gift of tongues. For example, Isaiah 28:11 and Joel 2:28 do not refer to the practice of speaking in unintelligible sounds. But the emphasis on the outpouring of the Holy Spirit is a central feature of New Testament religion. *All* of those present at the first Christian Pentecost were filled with the Holy Spirit (Acts 2:4) All who love and obey the Lord are to receive the Spirit. (John 14:15-17) Along with the Ephesian Christians we are enjoined to "be filled with the Spirit." (Ephesians 5:18) In this the neopentecostals and Wesley before them are right. The mainline churches have too often failed to give due emphasis to the work of the Holy Spirit in the hearts of believers.

149

But questions remain. Do the neopentecostals interpret the New Testament soundly? On the basis of what we have seen to be the biblical teaching (see Chapters 1, 2, and 3), we would have to say that the interpretations of neopentecostals on the Holy Spirit leave much to be desired.

They rightly hold that *some* Christians, particularly some at Corinth, spoke in unknown tongues. They are wrong when they make the gift of tongues, and the interpretation of them, *major signs of the Spirit's presence and power*.

• Anyone who reads carefully what Paul wrote to the Corinthians on this subject knows that Paul was trying to control a divisive, often fruitless, and at times dangerous practice. He was permissive toward it for those who practiced it at Corinth. He said, ". . . do not forbid speaking in tongues." (1 Corinthians 14:39) He even thanked God that he spoke in tongues more than any of them. (14:18) But he said this primarily so he could go on to say, ". . . nevertheless, in church I would rather speak five words with my mind, in order to instruct others, than ten thousand words in a tongue." (14:19) We can hardly imagine a stronger statement than that.

Moreover, we need to bear in mind Paul's example as a missionary to the other cities where he worked. We have no evidence that he went into any city (including Corinth) and encouraged people to speak in tongues. (See Acts 18:1-16.) It is true that at Ephesus, when he laid his hands on the twelve people involved, the Holy Spirit came on them "and they spoke with tongues and prophesied." (19:6) But when he taught those in the synagogue for three months, he was boldly arguing and pleading "about the kingdom of God" (19:8), with no mention of tongues. When Paul took the congregation out of the synagogue because of the opposition, he "argued daily" for two years "so that all the residents of Asia heard the word of the Lord." (19:10) Also, the list in Ephesians of the gifts of the risen Lord through the Spirit does not even mention tongues. (4:11)

Note that in the list of gifts in Paul's Letter to the Romans, written very late in his life, he made no mention of the gift of tongues. (12:6-8) To the Galatians, Ephesians, Philippians, Colossians, and Thessalonians Paul wrote nothing on speaking in tongues. Even in his writings that give counsel to individuals, he does not mention tongues. These facts imply that he did not regard speaking in tongues as essential either to the gospel or to a vital Christian experience.

On the basis of his letters we would have to say that Paul's interest in speaking in tongues was confined almost exclusively to the Christians at Corinth. His primary concern there was to hold the church together, for it tended to be torn to pieces by a divisive and sect-type spirit. In 1 Corinthians 12 through 14 Paul was obviously making a plea for unity in Christ and in Christian love.

● In referring to the gifts of the Spirit Paul placed speaking in tongues and interpreting tongues low on the list. (1 Corinthians 12:8-10, 28, 29-30) He pleaded with the Christians at Corinth to "desire the higher gifts." (12:31) In the great Chapter 13 Paul said that no matter what tongues a man spoke (even the tongues of angels), without love there was nothing but noise and clanging. So he wrote: "Make love your aim, and earnestly desire the spiritual gifts, especially that you may prophesy" (which means the gift of upbuilding and encouraging people in the church). (14:1, 3-4)

Paul's directives are to be permissive regarding speaking in tongues whenever the practice is not divisive and when it tends to express adoration of God, assurance, obedience, and joy in the Lord. But at best it is wholly secondary and unessential to receiving the power and presence of the Holy Spirit.

All Christians are to be united in their sense of fellowship in Jesus Christ and to be filled with his love. If, beyond this, they speak in tongues, let them do so for the most part in private or with a few friends. And let them avoid trying to change the rest of the church in ways not required by Jesus, Paul, or the New Testament in general. Let *all* in the church come together for worship, study, and work in mutual respect because of their unity in Christ. This is incomparably more important than any *special* gift of the Spirit.

Let those who now speak in tongues remember that the Spirit may lead them to give up that practice in the interest of guiding them to the higher levels of the Spirit's work. For some, speaking in tongues may be a gift or stage to be given up for a greater growth in grace. Indeed, some persons have reported that this has happened to them, and they rejoice in it. Or those who speak in tongues may continue to do so and still receive the greater gifts as well. Many have testified to this and backed up their witness with their lives in the church and in the world.

● To summarize, we may say that in Paul's writings as a whole, as well as in his missionary work, he never concentrated heavily on speaking in tongues. This was a side issue into which he was drawn by the special situation he encountered as a problem only among the Christians at Corinth.

When we put this with the fact that there are only two instances recorded in Acts of speaking in tongues (10:44-48; 19:2-7), we see further that this practice was merely incidental. (The reference in Acts 2:4 is a different matter, I believe, because it has to do with speaking in foreign languages that were clearly understood by those who knew those languages [2:5-11].) Many references in Acts mention the fullness of the Spirit or receiving the Spirit without any hint of speaking in tongues: 1:5, 8; 4:8, 31; 5:32; 6:3, 5; 8:14-19; 9:17-19; 11:15-16, 24; 13:9, 52; 15:8-9.

Furthermore, the Book of Hebrews makes no mention of speaking in tongues. The same is true of James; First and Second Peter; First, Second, and Third John; Jude; and the Book of Revelation.

● The final authority on matters of belief and practice for Christians is Jesus himself. Nowhere in the four Gospels (with the exception of Mark 16:9-20) did Jesus mention speaking in "new tongues." He did not teach his followers to expect it, nor did he refer to it as a gift of the Spirit. It would be unthinkable for Jesus to have failed to teach this if he had thought of it either as an important or a necessary gift of the Holy Spirit.

If Jesus had been interested in the gift of tongues, he would surely have said something about it in the context of John 15:26-27. What he said is that the Spirit would bear witness to him (Jesus). No mention is made of speaking in tongues.

Thus we see from the New Testament that Jesus himself made it impossible for his followers to concentrate heavily on speaking in tongues. His silence, along with that of the

writers of the four Gospels, speaks clearly enough for all to understand.

In the Light of the Christian Heritage

Christian history shows a recurring interest in being filled with the Holy Spirit. In all eras many Christians have felt the need for the power from God which the Spirit released at Pentecost. The Wesleyan revival in England is an instance of the passionate desire to recover the historic biblical emphasis on the power of the Holy Spirit. This is the primary motive back of the neopentecostal movement. The hope and prayer are for the new life in the Spirit. And this is good.

Yet the Christian churches throughout the centuries, in keeping with the spirit and example of Jesus and the basic directives of the New Testament, have steered clear of an emphasis on speaking in tongues. We have seen that the church repudiated Montanism, an early Christian movement that included glossolalia. We have seen also that for nearly fourteen centuries the practice of speaking in tongues died out almost altogether.

Moreover, even though speaking in tongues was, now and then, an accompanying factor in the great revivals of England and the United States, it was not the primary factor in them. Nor was it essential. As Hinson says, "There is no evidence to show, . . . that glossolalia preceded a revival." [1] In harmony with the spirit of Jesus, with his emphasis on the Holy Spirit as magnifying his own great work, and with the New Testament as a whole, speaking in tongues has

---

[1] *Speaking in Tongues*, Watson E. Mills, ed., pp. 72, 77.

not been viewed in historic Christianity as either very important or necessary.

More than this, when speaking in tongues has been practiced, the churches have often viewed it more as a problem than as an asset. This has been true up to recent times when the pentecostal churches were formed.

Even in the pentecostal churches, however, speaking in tongues is often seen to be secondary and not essential as a sign of the Spirit's presence. *The main goal for all Christians, including those who speak in tongues, is receiving power through the presence of the Spirit*—the Spirit of the living Christ. Those who speak in tongues readily agree to this.

The weight of evidence for nearly two thousand years of Christian history is against those who regard speaking in tongues as a primary feature of the Christian life. But, again, the church has tended to be permissive regarding it except when those who have practiced it have had the spirit of pride and divisiveness. Some of my friends who speak in tongues are eager to point out that those who are filled with pride and divisiveness have not experienced baptism with the Spirit.

In the Light of Practical Christian Living

Some errors or prejudices need to be corrected at the outset. Some people have said that those who speak in tongues tend to be emotionally unbalanced, hysterical, easily subject to hypnosis, and even schizophrenic. In addition, the charge has been made that they tend to be inadequate as persons —uncertain, socially maladjusted, cranky, anxious, and lacking in identity. *Recent studies have made it clear that these charges are not true.* Psychology is neither for nor against speaking in tongues. As far as Christians are concerned, psychology does not and cannot decide on the role of glossolalia in the churches.

● What are we to say on the basis of Christian experience? Millions of Christians have experienced the power or infilling of the Holy Spirit without speaking in tongues. Even at Corinth only a limited number did this. (1 Corinthians 12:30) Thus we see it is not essential. If speaking in tongues were a necessary sign of baptism in the Spirit, as we have seen, we would have to count Wesley out. Similarly, we would have to exclude nearly every first-rate mind and saint in Christian history. Note in this connection that Wesley and his followers among the English-speaking Methodists, as well as Otterbein, Albright, and their German-speaking counterparts in the United States, gave no encouragement to the notion that speaking in tongues is a primary or essential sign of baptism with the Holy Spirit.

● Is speaking in tongues a desirable practice? For a few it may be, for others, not. Experience teaches that if anyone speaks in tongues as the Spirit gives utterance, he should go ahead and do so. Indeed, he may not be able to hold back from doing so. (I would speak in tongues if I received the gift.) But this ought to be done primarily in the privacy of one's own soul or in small groups. For those who practice glossolalia, the genuine experience enables them to feel joy in the Lord, to adore, to feel assurance and submission, and to be renewed within. *It is their prayer-language when all other words fail.* They claim a new affection and new power for creative living.

For this reason those who do not speak in tongues and do not feel the desire to do so *should respect and appreciate* those who do. We should remember with gratitude that the neopentecostals, in contrast to many of their forerunners in this century, are not anti-intellectual, antichurch, and anti-culture. The main point is that all genuine Christians will work together to magnify Jesus Christ as Lord in their hearts, in the community of faith, and in the world. We must never forget that the church at Corinth is a perpetual reminder that the special gifts of the Spirit are no guarantee of the greater gifts of faith, hope, and love.

● But more remains to be said. On the basis of experience can we say that those who speak in tongues have been or are among the great dynamic leaders of Christian history or of Christian saintliness? Are ministers made more effective and lay persons more truly dedicated in their Christian witness? Except for Paul—who made little mention of speaking in tongues as a resource for Christian living—who can be named among the outstanding leaders? Tertullian was one. The Christians of great energy and achievement—Irenaeus, Chrysostom, Augustine, Aquinas, Luther, Calvin, Wesley, Asbury, Otterbein, Albright, Moody, Mott, Kagawa, Schweitzer, Helen Kim, others—either did not speak in tongues or regarded it as unimportant. They were persons of great energy and dynamic leadership. If the greatest Christians have not received their power from this gift, then we cannot commend it as an important resource for creative Christian leadership.

All these Christians received the power from the presence of the Holy Spirit without the gift of tongues. Moreover, we have reason to believe that, for many people, speaking in tongues seems old-fashioned *and lacks the power to renew in the ongoing of the Christian life.* Unintelligible utterances, even when interpreted, are not normally means of Christian growth. As Wesley knew so well, *unless we tap the primary sources of growth in grace, we stagnate,* we die on the vine.

Nevertheless, many Christians have found a new sense of commitment and power that came to a focus when they began to speak in tongues. For them the Spirit is the source of power, but tongues have given them a sign of the Spirit's presence. They had a new desire to study the Bible, to engage in intercessory prayer, to serve the church, and to help others. This is to the good and to their credit.

● Experience teaches us, however, that any undue emphasis on tongues has recurring dangers. One is the danger of fake and fraud, as suggested under "Some Problems" in Chapter 14. Those who speak in tongues are among the first to admit this. Some people even guarantee that with the payment of a fee and certain procedures people will break forth in tongues. Others try to induce the practice by telling a person each move to make—setting the jaw, manipulating the lips, and the like. This turns Christianity into a cheap fraud.

Some have said that the practice of speaking in tongues may be authentic or phony. It may be merely psychological, or it may be of demons or of the Devil or of the Spirit. It is not always easy to know which. Therefore, the scriptural warning to test and to prove the spirit to see whether or not it is of God becomes specially relevant. (1 John 4:1-3a) What better ways of testing are there than through prayerful reflections on the guidelines of Scripture, tradition, Christian experience, and reason?

Experience in the local churches reveals also a constant danger of divisiveness and self-righteousness of the sect-type way of thinking. Some who speak in tongues feel that God has shown them that he accepts them and blessees them by this gift. When others do not have this gift, pride and selfishness lead to a judgmental attitude toward fellow Christians. They regard those others as, at best, second-class Christians or, at worst, no Christians at all. In this way, speaking in tongues turns into an instrument of the Devil. Pride, selfishness, haughtiness, and the consequent divisiveness, under whatever guise, are anti-Christ. Would any Christian give Jesus a low rating because he did not speak in tongues?

On the other side, Christians in local churches who do not speak in tongues are likely to have harsh and judgmental attitudes toward those who do. This too is deplorable. The great need is for love, mutual respect, and cooperation in the Lord's work.

● In these days when there are so many versions of the Bible—with the Psalms and other great passages, so many hymns, so many good written materials, so much good poetry and music, most Christians may find that the best ways to adore, to rejoice in the Lord, are not through unintelligible sounds, but through reciting great verses, singing inspired hymns, using a vocabulary enriched by the great prayers of the community of faith. Consequently, every church should make available abundant resources for celebrating our overwhelming joy in the Lord.

In any event, as in all matters that do not strike at the root of Christianity, let us live and let live, think and let think, feel and let feel, and then work together in the fellowship of faith for the glory of God and benefit of persons.

The Holy Spirit and Divine Healing, Exorcism, Psychic Phenomena, And the Occult

This symbol was used in exorcism rituals in the twelfth century but was used later as a decorative cross.

Divine Healing

From the earliest times the history of Christianity has included a continuing interest in God's healing presence. It is a part of the universal Christian heritage. In addition, whenever the power of the Holy Spirit has been emphasized, people have had a tendency to believe in divine healing.

The Christian Science movement, though not based on the biblical directives concerning the Holy Spirit, makes divine healing a central feature of its teaching and practice. In the contemporary charismatic movement, or neo-pentecostalism, services of healing are not uncommon. Sometimes thousands of people will come together either to be healed or to watch as the healing services progress. Many people have claimed to be healed. Neopentecostals have a general openness toward God's power to heal all sorts of ailments, including so-called "incurable" diseases.

Against this background of the past and present, what are we to say about the Holy Spirit and divine healing? The community of faith, lay persons and ministers, need to respond to this question in the light of Scripture, tradition, Christian experience, and common sense.

Four Aspects to Be Considered

● *First,* the belief in divine healing has a *biblical basis.* Long before the coming of Jesus Christ, the belief in divine healing was a part of the Hebrew heritage. It took on new dimensions in Jesus' ministry. As far as we know, Jesus never spoke in tongues, but he healed people. This ministry of healing was not merely an incidental or accidental part of his lifework. On some occasions he healed great numbers of people who were brought to him. (See Mark 1:32-34.) He did not wait for them to come to him; he went out among them and cured all sorts of diseases. (Matthew 4: 23) The writers of the four Gospels will not let us forget the picture of Jesus as the great physician, for that is the way they saw and remembered him. We know from the Gospels many truths about Jesus; but few facts are more clearly evident than that he healed people with all sorts of diseases.

The lepers, the blind and deaf, the crippled, the handicapped, the diseased, the mentally disarranged—all these were blessed by the Master's healing ministry. This reveals for all time God's never ending concern for the physical health and mental well-being of his children.

One dimension of Jesus' ministry was giving people healthy and normal bodies. In this regard his ministry stands forever against those notions that diseases and handicaps are sent by God because of the sins of parents, because of a reincarnation from a previous state, and the like. Jesus never forgot that human suffering and pain are tragic, even in the sight of God. Jesus' great heart always responded to the cries of suffering people. This was one of the sure signs that with his coming the kingdom of God was at hand.

Jesus also gave his twelve disciples the power to cure diseases, and he sent them out to preach the good news of the Kingdom and to heal people. (Luke 9:1-2) He commanded the seventy to heal the sick. (10:9)

After Jesus' death and resurrection, through the Holy Spirit some of the apostles were given the power to heal. Though this was not a central feature of their ministry, as it had been with Jesus, it was at least one dimension. Paul viewed the power to heal as a special gift of the Holy Spirit. (1 Corinithians 12:9, 30) And this was a widely accepted belief among the earliest Christians.

● *Second,* against this background we might suppose that the *community of faith* would have given a central place to the Holy Spirit's special gift of divine healing. But, except for certain groups, this has not been the case. The church still believes that some people are given the power to become agents of divine healing, but the Holy Spirit's special gift of healing is neither essential nor primary in the life of the community of faith.

This belief is in keeping with the New Testament itself. There the special gift of healing was for a limited few, although all Christians have been concerned for the sick and handicapped. Their prayers and deeds have reflected this attitude. The primary manifestation of the Holy Spirit in the community of faith in regard to healing has been not in special gifts of healing but *in the Christlike concern that has led to the building of hospitals and homes where doctors and nurses can do their special work.*

Christians understand God as One who cares for his children. As Jesus demonstrated, the Father wants to restore the sick and handicapped to health and normalcy. Christians have prayed for God's healing power to be felt by the sick. A note of expectancy has always been expressed in the intercessory prayers of Christians for divine healing. Christians will and should continue to pray for the physical and mental health of one another and of all in need.

● *Third,* the belief in divine healing as a special gift to some persons need not undermine our confidence in medi-

161

cal science. Physicians, psychiatrists, dentists, nurses, and all those connected with hospitals and nursing homes are engaged in *ministries of healing*. Indeed, Christians understand that all these persons, when they do their work well, are God's instruments to aid the sick and handicapped.

To be sure, a few sects of Christians believe that such medical help should never be accepted. According to them, this would show a lack of faith in God's special healing power. But this is not characteristic of the Christian community as a whole. In fact, the church's confidence in modern medicine is abundantly evident in the number of first-rate hospitals established and expanded under the sponsorship of Christians, for they believe that God heals through the knowledge gained in medical studies and through the skills of physicians. In a true sense, all healing is divine healing.

We see that both the church at large and the more responsible persons who claim the Holy Spirit's gift of healing not only affirm medical science, they support it and seek confirmation from it.

● The belief in God's special acts of healing is made more plausible, even in this age of science, by the influences of the mind or spirit on the body. Physicians have long known that the mind affects the healing processes of the body. Psychosomatic medicine (pertaining to mind-body interaction) seems to be here to stay. It tends to support the *possibility* that God can enter into these processes and heal "incurable" diseases.

Everyone knows persons who have claimed that God healed them without the aid of medical science. In some cases those with "incurable" diseases have been suddenly restored to complete health during services of divine healing. Scientific studies have confirmed the validity of many of these claims. The vast majority of reports of divine healing may be unconfirmed, but even the most hard-nosed scientific realists have found that in at least 10 per cent of the cases the claims were valid. That is, the symptoms of medically "incurable" diseases disappeared through the prayers and actions of persons claiming that God used them to heal. This has happened also in small groups where earnest prayers of intercession have been offered up in faith with the laying-on of hands.

We have, then, biblical, historical, and practical grounds for believing in these special acts of divine healing. By no means is it impossible that even today God's healing acts occur through a limited number of persons who have received the gift of healing through the Holy Spirit.

● *Fourth*, the church as a whole, however, has never laid great emphasis on the special gifts and acts of divine healing. In addition to the New Testament directives, which do not make this the heart of the gospel, other factors have been at work.

Christians have long been aware of certain dangers in stressing the Holy Spirit's special acts of healing. Experience has taught that the claims of divine healing are often phony. Also, people in desperate need have been exploited frequently and have been given false hopes. They have been deceived into expecting miracles that did not happen. Some who have claimed to have the Spirit's special gift of healing have simply had unusual hypnotic powers that may or may not express God's acts of healing.

The church has known also that we do not understand the laws of divine healing. Why is the gift of healing bestowed on some and not on others? We do not know. Why are a few healed and the vast majority not? Nobody knows. The explanation, "Because some had faith and others did not," does not make sense. Some with the strongest faith have died prematurely from "incurable" diseases. And some who seemed to have a weak faith have been healed. Why? The community of faith does not profess to know. A famous contemporary healer said, "You ask me why everyone is not healed. I don't know. If you think you have questions, I have more."

Because the Spirit's special acts of healing are not at the center of the biblical teaching on the church's mission and because of these other factors, *the church has never allowed the practice of divine healing to become either basic or central*. At the center is always the gospel of God's forgiving and empowering grace through Jesus Christ. The Holy Spirit authorizes and confirms this primary mission of the community of faith. Sin, ineffectiveness, and death remain the major concerns with which the Holy Spirit deals. We believe that Christ died to save sinners; all else is secondary.

The Holy Spirit and Health

We should remember that whenever the Holy Spirit works redemptively in us, we become aware of certain mysterious health-giving processes. The tendency toward physical and mental health is present in those whose sins are forgiven and who are receptive to Christ's love whereby they love their fellow human beings.

The main point is to keep our minds and hearts on Jesus Christ and his power to redeem. In addition, as an attending influence, *the movement of our bodily processes is toward health through faith in Jesus Christ*. Then the healing powers of souls redeemed by the living Christ will be felt in the widely differing ranges of service to our fellow human beings. As far as the healing ministry is concerned, the Christlike concern of Christians is expressed *through intercessory prayers on the one hand and through physicians, nurses, orderlies, hospitals, and nursing homes on the other*.

Satan, Demons, and Exorcism

Demons and Exorcism

Exorcism is the practice of driving out demons by means of prayer, laying-on of hands, commands, and other ceremonial acts. It is based on the belief that, in some cases, deep personality disturbances are caused by demon possession. Demons are said to take over a person's soul and body and dominate it for evil purposes. Moreover, according to this belief, the person is so thoroughly under the sway of a demon or demons as to be powerless to control his or her behavior. Consequently, according to some, an individual or group is needed to serve as divinely appointed agents of exorcism. But the the practice of exorcism is very limited among Christians.

● In primitive religions, such as shamanism, exorcism is a central feature of religious practice. I recall that when I was a boy in Korea I saw many exorcists at work. In those days the non-Christian masses held a widespread belief that human life was surrounded by spirits, most of whom were evil. In particular, diseases were caused by evil spirits. The cure was to be found in getting rid of those spirits. How? By means of at least three kinds of processes.

One method was to let the evil spirits out of the body

by inserting a large needle where the pain was the most severe. The demon or evil spirit could then slip out through the hole made by the needle. Another method was to get rid of the evil spirit by cajoling and persuading it to leave. The third method was to frighten the evil spirits and drive them out by all sorts of noises, contortions, hexes, ceremonies, and so on. Often all three methods were used. Exorcism in one form or another has been practiced extensively in primitive religions in many parts of the world.

● The belief in devils and demons has not been confined to primitive religions. In surprising ways this belief and the practices based on it have appeared on the modern scene. Among some Christians the practice of exorcism claims a biblical basis. Jesus was said to have cast out demons. Some of the apostles did so also.

As members of the community of faith, how are we to think about demons and exorcism? Several comments are indicated.

In New Testament times the words used to name diseases were vastly different from those we use today. Emotionally disturbed and psychotic persons were said to be possessed by demons. Psychoanalysis and psychiatry were nearly two thousands years away. Naturally one supposed that people who were distraught, violent toward themselves and others, were under the power of some awful demonic force. In any event, this is the way the demonic condition of certain people was interpreted. Jesus cured them by putting them in their right minds.

More is involved here than names of mental disorders. The Gospel writers indicate in some instances that real spirits or forces possessed certain people and that those forces were "driven out." Most of us do not believe in the existence of demons. We can account for nearly every mental disarrangement without reference to them. Body chemistry, heredity, physiological deficiencies, subconscious processes, resentment, hostility, anxiety, and unfortunate circumstances would seem to serve as adequate explanations of most mental disturbances. The only question that remains is, Might there not be, in some cases, such twists and perversities of mind as would indicate demon-possession? Those who practice exorcism would say Yes.

● Demon-possession may be left as an open question. It

is at least *theoretically* possible—that is, one can believe without contradiction—that evil spirits exist and that they take possession of certain individuals. This is one reason the church has never denied the possibility of demon-possession. We have some reason to believe that evil forces of certain kinds that are more powerful than people may exert sinister influences on individuals. Yet the church has not, in any basic way, regarded the practice of exorcism as a special manifestation of the Holy Spirit. This whole way of thought and practice has been at best a side issue and at worst a gross delusion.

At this point, again, Wesley's attitude and practice are illuminating. On one occasion he was accused of being an exorcist. Two women were, as he believed, tormented by the Devil. He and many others prayed for them, and they were "delivered." "But," asks Wesley, "where meantime were 'the exorcisms in form, according to the Roman fashion'? I never used them; I never saw them; I know nothing about them." [1] It is one thing to pray for and with people; but it is another thing to engage in rituals and practices of exorcism.

Some Real Dangers

During the present century Christian people have not given much importance to demons and exorcism. They have tended to regard these as essentially superstitious. They have been aware that people who emphasize the existence of demons and the practice of exorcism are likely to adopt ideas and practices that are contrary to the Bible.

---

[1] *Letters*, IV, 345.

These people tend to lose sight of the biblical teaching on the *unique mission* of the Holy Spirit, and they obscure the basic teaching on the sovereignty of God. For example, some people suppose that Satan, with his army of demons, can rival God himself. They fear that Satan poses a real threat to God's reign and consequently to the ultimate triumph of righteousness.

● This is contrary to biblical teaching. In revealed religion nothing, not even the sum total of all creatures, can pose any real threat to God. He alone is sovereign. He alone is perfect. He alone *has* to be. All else may or may not be. All the "powers and principalities" of evil are trivial compared to the unutterable greatness of God.

We may not agree altogether with Luther's ideas, but we do affirm with him God's absolute sway over all evil forces when he said:

> "And though this world, with devils filled,
>   Should threaten to undo us,
> We will not fear, for God hath willed
>   His truth to triumph through us;
> The Prince of Darkness grim—
>   We tremble not for him;
> His rage we can endure,
>   For lo, his doom is sure;
> One little word shall fell him." [2]

The biblical teaching is that God's grace in Jesus Christ, made available through the Holy Spirit, enables us to become more than conquerors over sin and evil. No evil forces have any sway over the Holy Spirit.

● What happens, of course, is that people often feel themselves threatened by evils within and without. They are victims of destructive habits that they cannot control. They deal with people who seem possessed by some demonic power that makes them selfish, mean, vengeful, or petty. Alcoholism and other forms of drug addiction, fears and phobias, crime, frustration, prejudice, laziness, inhumanity ——these and numberless other evils—overwhelm people.

---

[2] From "A Mighty Fortress Is Our God," *The Book of Hymns* (*The Methodist Hymnal*) No. 20 and *The Hymnal* (E.U.B.) No. 59.

They feel that they are under the sway of some awesome evil power or powers beyond themselves.

Evil

Our culture seems to have a mysterious fascination with evil. Maximilian Rudwin, in his book entitled *The Devil in Legend and Literature*,[3] describes something of this fascination as it has manifested itself across several thousand years. For example, Dante's portrayal of hell has been far more fascinating than his vision of heaven. This led one writer to say, "If Dante's great poem had been a description of heaven, no one would read it. The interest centers in hell and purgatory." The medieval mind tormented itself with obsessive pictures of hell, demons, and evil forces. All sorts of guesses were made as to the number and variety of demons. In 1563 Johannes Wierus said that there were 7,405,926 devils and that there was no possibility of error in his calculations. A professor at Basle estimated that there were over two and a half trillion devils. A medieval monk said that their number exceeds calculation since it is equal to the number of grains of sand in the sea. John Milton's Satan, and not God, is the real hero of *Paradise Lost*.

We could multiply tales, stories, legends, and accounts in literature, examples in sculpture and art concerning the number, the names, and the acts of demons. No useful purpose would be served by doing so here. But we may note in passing that Christian history itself has a disastrous tendency to view even fellow Christians as instruments of the Devil. The Roman Catholics regarded the Waldensians, the Huguenots, and many others as led astray by the Devil. Luther and other Protestants viewed the Pope and Catholic clergymen as the Devil's priests. They saw the Turks and others who were outside the body of Christ as instruments of Satan. We are not very far removed from the days of witch hunts.

This is a long, pathetic, and tragic story within the general domain of Christian history. It illustrates how far the pride, ignorance, and superstition of people can carry them from the revelation of God in Jesus Christ. For this reason,

---

[3] Open Court Publishing Company, 1959.

without a clear, persistent, and full reliance on the basic directives of Scripture, we are almost sure to go wrong.

● Let us not suppose that modern people are free from obsessions with inner and outer evils. The vocabulary of psychoanalysis is full of them. Along with a realistic orientation toward the stark dread realities of human nature, we find evidence also of depressive fascination with the evils in people. Often these evils are so disconnected from man's responsible freedom and from divine grace as to make repentance irrelevant. Guilt becomes a "complex" rather than a responsibility before God and humankind for inner and outer badness.

Contemporary drama portrays on stage, screen, and television every conceivable variety of crime, cruelty, horror, psychological imbalance, frustration, and sin—all for public consumption. People of our time may be said to be obsessed with evils and demonic forces of all sorts. What may be just as tragic is the fact that so few Christians are willing or able to amass an adequate protest to the garbage served up by mass media. Consequently, in this age of science and technology we find a renewed interest in the occult, with sporadic excursions into demonology and exorcism. Satanism too is not merely a word: It has its devotees today as it did in the past.

Once again we are reminded of the saying, "It is unbelievable what people will believe."

● In much of this interest in demons, if not nearly all of it, the gospel is overshadowed by man's obsessions and despair. God's power to redeem people and to enable them, by grace, to rise above all obsessive fears of evil forces—that power is too often made null and void by the superstitions of people. Consequently, the work of the Holy Spirit is obscured and even implicitly denied.

The main idea to remember is that God has acted mightily in Jesus Christ to forgive our sins and, by the power of the Holy Spirit, to re-create our souls through the new life in Jesus Christ within the community of faith.

Psychic Phenomena

Under the term *psychic phenomena* we have in mind several areas of thought. One is mental telepathy, the ability to read the minds of people while absent from them; extrasensory perception is noted in many other forms. Another area is the supposed ability to manipulate plants and inanimate objects through the powers of the mind. Still another is that of predicting certain events.

● The important question is, *What does the Holy Spirit have to do with these phenomena?* We are not interested here in affirming or denying their reality. Credible scholarly studies are being carried on in an effort to understand them. Whatever the outcome of these studies, one truth remains clear: The Holy Spirit's primary mission is not telepathic communication or extrasensory perception or the power to change physical bodies (such as bending a nail by mental action) or to predict certain secular events. All this misses the unique work of the Holy Spirit in magnifying Jesus Christ as Lord and Redeemer in and through the community of faith.

Some people imagine that the power to predict nonreligious events, such as the assassination of President John F. Kennedy, reveals unusually close ties with the Holy Spirit. Indeed, some have suggested that such a power is a gift of the Holy Spirit. I have no desire to deny the possibility of unusual powers of prediction whenever the conditions for events are set up. But we have no reason to connect this with the activity of the Holy Spirit. People may have unusual powers in many lines, such as art, literature, music, business, personal relations, psychic phenomena. Why should these be linked with the Holy Spirit? To do so is, again, to miss the biblical teaching on this subject. It misguides people as to the realities and joys of Christian experience for they may be so fascinated with certain sensational or unusual manifestations of psychic phenomena as to become deaf to the call of the Spirit.

Spiritualism

What about spiritualism? This is the belief in and practice of communicating with the dead. Christians do not deny the possibility of this. But they view it as outside the sphere of the biblical revelation. They know, too, of the constant danger of lapsing into superstitious notions about communicating with the dead. Moreover, because of the close ties of memory with departed loved ones, people are often exploited and deceived. Also, nearly all the supposed "communications" are so trivial as to be unworthy of serious attention. They do not tell us what we most want to know.

In any event, spiritualism is not a part of the Christian religion. It was neither taught nor practiced by Jesus and the apostles. Christians stress the life after death as the soul's continued existence in the new dimension of the kingdom of heaven. Even as they live constructively here, they look forward to the renewed glorious fellowship in heaven with those who have passed away.

Astrology

Astrology is the belief that a person's life is in some fundamental way governed by the stars. It consists mainly of an elaborate system of ideas linking the birthdays and birth months with various constellations.

Astrology is not only nonbiblical, it is antibiblical. It implies fatalistic elements. The Bible teaches that no one's life is under the sway of the stars. Every human being is summoned to respond to God and to live under his sway. Therefore, Christians view astrology as another superstition that has no legitimate place among thoughtful people. That the Holy Spirit repudiates this ancient superstition is self-evident. If a person has freedom of choice, astrology is laid aside. Freedom to decide is an experienced reality.

We recognize, of course, that some psychological values may be gained by the tidbits of good advice about keeping calm, about handling an unpleasant event, and so forth. But this is trivial in the extreme compared to what is available to Christians through devotional literature and habits of cultivating the devotional life.

Selected Resources

A. KEY PASSAGES OF SCRIPTURE

1. Old Testament
Genesis 1:1-2
Numbers 11:16-17
1 Samuel 16:11-13
2 Samuel 23:1-2
Job 33:4; 34:14
Psalms 33:6; 51:10-12; 104:28-30; 139:1-12, 23-24; 143-10
Isaiah 30:1-2; 40:28-31; 61:1-2; 63:7-14
Jeremiah 11 through 20; 23
Ezekiel 2:2-3; 8:3; 11:1-5; 36:25-28; 37:1-14
Joel 2:21-29
Micah 3:8
Zechariah 4:6; 7:12

2. New Testament
Matthew 28:16-20
Luke 3:15-16, 21-22; 24:45-53
John 3:1-8, 34; 7:32-39; 14:25-26; 15:26; 16:7-15; 17:12-21
Acts 1:4-8; 2; 10; 13:1-39
Romans 8
1 Corinthians 12 through 14
2 Corinthians 5:5-7, 17
Galatians 5:5-25
1 John 4

B. SELECTED BOOKS

1. Books for the General Reader

Bach, Marcus, *The Inner Ecstasy: The Power and the Glory of Speaking in Tongues*. Nashville: Abingdon Press, 1971. Apex edition.

Harkness, Georgia, *The Fellowship of the Holy Spirit*. Nashville: Abingdon Press, 1966.*

Hunt, Earl G., Jr., ed. *Storms and Starlight: Bishops' Messages on the Holy Spirit*. Nashville: Tidings, 1974.

Jorstad, Erling, ed. *The Holy Spirit in Today's Church: A Handbook of the New Pentecostalism*. Nashville: Abingdon Press, 1973. Contains a carefully selected list of books and denominational statements.

Kildahl, John P., *The Psychology of Speaking in Tongues*. New York: Harper & Row, 1972. Contains an extensive list of books and articles on glossolalia, or speaking in tongues.

Kinghorn, Kenneth Cain, *Fresh Wind of the Spirit*. Nashville: Abingdon Press, 1975.

Kuhlman, Kathryn, *God Can Do It Again*. Englewood Cliffs, N. J.: Prentice-Hall, Inc., 1969. (For an excellent

---

* Out of print.

brief evaluation of long-range results of a healing service in Minneapolis, see William A. Nolan, M.D., "In Search of a Miracle," in *McCall's,* September 1974, pp. 82-83, 101-2, 104, 106-7.)

Mills, Watson, ed. *Speaking in Tongues: Let's Talk About It.* Waco, Texas: Word Books, 1973. Contains an excellent list of books and articles.

O'Connor, Edward D., *The Pentecostal Movement in the Catholic Church.* Notre Dame: Ave Maria Press, 1971.

Pittenger, Norman, *The Holy Spirit.* Philadelphia: United Church Press, 1974.

Richards, W. T. H., *Pentecost Is Dynamite.* Nashville: Abingdon Press, 1974.

Rudwin, Maximilian, *The Devil in Legend and Literature.* LaSalle, Ill.: Open Court Publishing Company, 1973.

Stokes, Mack B., *Major United Methodist Beliefs,* revised and enlarged. Nashville: Abingdon Press, 1971. Chapter V.

—————————, *The Bible and Modern Doubt.* Old Tappan, N. J.: Fleming H. Revell Company, 1970. Chapter 10.

Taylor, John V., *The Go-Between God: The Holy Spirit on the Christian Mission.* Philadelphia: Fortress Press, 1973.

Tuttle, Robert G., Jr., *The Partakers.* Nashville: Abingdon Press, 1974.

Van Dusen, Henry P., *Spirit, Son and Father.* New York: Charles Scribner's Sons, 1958.*

Walker, Alan, *Breakthrough: Rediscovery of the Holy Spirit.* Nashville: Abingdon Press, 1969.

Weaver, Horace R., and Hares, James C., *Channels of His Spirit.* Nashville: Abingdon Press, 1973.

Wesley, John, "A Plain Account of Christian Perfection" in *The Works of John Wesley.* Grand Rapids, Mich.: Zondervan Publishing Company, n.d., Volume XI, pp. 366-446. (See also Wesley's sermon "The Circumcision of the Heart" which, though his earliest publication, he continued to adhere to throughout his life.)*

The Work of the Holy Spirit, Report of the Special Committee. The General Assembly of the Presbyterian Church in the United States of America, Room 1201 475 Riverside Drive, New York, N.Y., 10027; 1970.

2. Books for More Advanced Study

Barrett, C. K., *The Holy Spirit and the Gospel Tradition.* Naperville, Ill.: Alec R. Allenson, Inc., 1966.

Hendry, George S., *The Holy Spirit in Christian Theology,* revised and enlarged. Philadelphia: Westminster Press, 1965.*

Kelsey, Morton T., *Healing and Christianity in Ancient Thought and Modern Times.* New York: Harper & Row, 1972.

Kirkpatrick, Dow, ed., *The Holy Spirit.* Nashville: Tidings, 1974.

Kuyper, Abraham, *The Work of the Holy Spirit,* translated from the Dutch by Henri De Vries. Grand Rapids, Mich.: Wm. B. Eerdmans, 1956.

Lampe, G. W. H., *The Seal of the Spirit: A Study in the Doctrine of Baptism and Confirmation in the New Testament and the Fathers.* Naperville, Ill.: Alec R. Allenson, Inc., 1967.

Lindstrom, Harald, *Wesley and Sanctification.* London: Epworth Press.*

Robinson, H. Wheeler, *The Christian Experience of the Holy Spirit.* London: Collins Fontana Paperbacks, 1962.*

Starkey, Lycurgus M., *The Work of the Holy Spirit: A Study in Wesleyan Theology.* Nashville: Abingdon Press, 1962.*

Stokes, Mack B., *The Epic of Revelation.* New York: McGraw-Hill, 1961. Chapter IX.*

Synan, Vinson, *The Holiness-Pentecostal Movement in the United States.* Grand Rapids, Mich.: Wm. B. Eerdmans, 1972.